The Legacy of the Bolshevik Revolution

EDITED BY
EDDIE ABRAHAMS

COUNTERATTACK · 1

First Published 1992

Larkin Publications
BCM Box 5909 London WC1N 3XX

© Larkin Publications

British Library Cataloguing in Publication Data
A catalogue record for this book is available from the British Library

ISBN 0905400 14 3

Typeset in Bembo and Univers
by Boldface Typesetting & Design
Printed by A Wheaton & Co Ltd, Exeter and London

Contents

PART THREE

Counter-revolution in the Soviet Union 1991

PART FOUR

Cuba resists!

PART FIVE
Uphold the banner of Communism!

Preface

Most of the material in this book first appeared as articles in *Fight Racism! Fight Imperialism!*, newspaper of the Revolutionary Communist Group, during 1989-1991 and the early part of 1992. Together they provide a clear materialist and class context in which to understand the crisis of socialism after the collapse of the socialist bloc and the lessons to be learned by a new communist movement.

The Legacy of the Bolshevik Revolution records all the principle political, economic and social features and developments during that dramatic period. There are, of course, chronological gaps and many facts and details, more or less significant for historians, are not recorded. This is inevitable given the original character of the material – theoretical and political commentaries for a bi-monthly publication.

This book is a contribution towards a discussion which is a necessary condition for the recovery and rejuvenation of the international communist movement.

EDDIE ABRAHAMS, JUNE 1992

Revolutionary retreats

The working class and anti-imperialist movement is experiencing its severest crisis since the collapse of the Second International in 1914. Among the poor and oppressed, where the socialist and Marxist banner was once prominent, we now hear the slogans of social democracy, reactionary nationalism and religious fundamentalism. In many instances, when the working class acts as a political force, it does so at the behest of hostile and reactionary classes.

The retreat and turmoil of the socialist and anti-imperialist movement was expressed most acutely in the dramatic collapse of the socialist bloc. A lengthy process of decline culminated in the rapid collapse of Eastern Europe in 1989. It reached its peak in August 1991 with Yeltsin's counter-coup in the USSR and the dissolution of the Soviet Union in December of that year. As a result, in most Eastern European countries and ex-Soviet republics, virulently anti-working class regimes are in power. Their mission is to secure the final subordination of the ex-socialist bloc's wealth and labour to imperialist capital, whilst consigning the majority of their peoples to unprecedented poverty.

As a direct consequence of these developments imperialism is confidently intensifying its war of destruction against the surviving socialist states of Cuba, Vietnam, China and Korea. Across the globe anti-imperialist movements have been forced into dangerous compromises with imperialism and its regional allies. In Angola and Mozambique, in Nicaragua and Cambodia anti-imperialist governments are being compelled to cede positions to pro-capitalists. The revolutionary government of Afghanistan which secured enormous advances for the Afghan people has finally been overwhelmed by the US-armed and financed Mojaheddin. Hailed as 'freedom fighters' by Reagan and Thatcher these fascists specialised in the destruction of schools, hospitals and clinics; they specialised in skinning alive captured Soviet soldiers. In power they will impose once again a regime of servitude and bondage upon the people of the country, and upon women in particular. Within the liberation movements in Palestine, Central America, South Africa, Ireland, the Basque country, the Philippines and elsewhere bourgeois and social democratic trends are growing in confidence.

The Reagan/Thatcher counter-revolution of the 1980s which so assiduously fought to reverse the tide of socialist and anti-imperialist advance has declared itself victorious. An epoch of revolutionary progress which stretched from 1917 to the 1959 Cuban Revolution, the historic 1975 defeat of the USA in Vietnam and the triumph of the Sandinistas in Nicaragua in 1979 appears to have closed. With the collapse of the socialist bloc we are witnessing the defeat of the first sustained effort to build societies free of capitalist exploitation. No wonder the sigh of bourgeois relief still reverberates so strongly: they believe they have vanquished the spectre of communism. That vision of progress which accompanied the Russian Revolution, that optimism which promised the elimination of capitalist and imperialist exploitation, poverty and suffering has been overshadowed by terrible defeats and disintegration.

In defence of scientific socialism

The overwhelming majority of British socialists welcomed developments in Eastern Europe and the ex-USSR claiming they were popular revolutions. With few exceptions, they proved to be incapable of examining developments from a Marxist standpoint, from the standpoint of the material interests of the mass of the working class. Captivated by the sight of 'mass movements' in Eastern Europe they turned a blind eye to the class forces which led these movements.

Mesmerised by the 'democratic slogans' of the 'revolution', they ignored its class character. They refused to condemn the pro-capitalist and pro-imperialist class forces, which concealed their real bourgeois material interests behind demands for freedom and democracy.

Fight Racism! Fight Imperialism! adopted a diametrically opposite standpoint. In numerous articles we argued that developments in the socialist bloc were 'a massive blow to the international working class and to the vast majority of humanity.' In a period when many a socialist and once-Marxist intellectual is making an embarrassed dash from previous standpoints, we offer these articles as examples of a materialist, realist, class analysis of what has turned out to be a counter-revolution of historic significance.

But an even broader purpose is served by this pamphlet. It is intended as a contribution in defence of scientific socialism, in defence of Marxism and the legacy of Leninism and the Russian Revolution. The onset of a profound international economic crisis will systematically undermine bourgeois claims about the superiority of capitalism. The bourgeois intelligentsia is therefore working hard to 'definitively' discredit and 'refute' Marxism. It must try rapidly to bury an ideology and experience which, embodying all that is progressive in human culture, provides the foundation for future working class progress.

The Bolshevik effort

A major weapon in the bourgeois arsenal against Marxism and communism will be the failure of the Russian Revolution. Enemies of the people and of socialism will seize on every weakness, every error, every blunder and every crime to present it as a 'deviation from civilization' and from the 'norms of decent human relations'. A central theme of their argument is that democracy and communism are not compatible; that democracy and a centrally planned economy are a contradiction in terms. They claim that the seizure of political power by the working class under the leadership of a 'Bolshevik' party will inevitably lead to tyranny. A new corrupt and privileged elite will then preside over an inherently faulty economy with no hope of matching the advances of market economies. The Soviet experience and its collapse is offered as their evidence.

Within the USSR a privileged elite did develop and eventually seized control of the Communist Party of the Soviet Union. (Note however that the most privileged have been the greatest enthusiasts for the market economy!) It is also beyond dispute that by the late 1970s the Soviet economy was in crisis, lagging far behind capitalism in labour productivity and the provision of consumer goods and services. These problems were compounded by the absence of proletarian democracy. As a result the working class was marginalised as a political force and its enthusiasm for socialism sapped. Power then passed effectively to anti-socialist trends.

But none of these problems were 'automatically' or 'naturally' generated by the expropriation of private capital, the organisation of a planned economy or the existence of a Bolshevik party. A planned economy expresses relations of social production in which the means of production and its benefits belong, not to individuals but to all. It is the antithesis of the market economy which expresses relations of social production in which the means of production and their benefits are the property of a tiny minority. Only narrow minded bourgeois prejudice, blind to the conditions of the majority of the world's population, could consider a planned economy as inherently unnatural or unworkable while hailing the market as fundamentally flawless!

To understand the problems and failures of the Bolshevik Revolution, Marxists consider the objective historical conditions in which it developed: the imperialist encirclement of the USSR and its relentless military, economic and political assault against it. This unceasing blockade and isolation prevented any sustained attempt to develop and advance the socialist planned economy. Over the decades this took its toll, generating and fostering reactionary trends within Soviet society and the CPSU in particular.

Starting from a semi-feudal base, the Soviet Union had no opportunity to catch up economically with the most advanced imperialist countries. First the Civil War and foreign intervention (1918-21) and then the Nazi invasion and war (1941-45) repeatedly devastated its economic base. A comprehensive imperialist economic boycott prevented the USSR from participating in the world-wide division of labour or benefiting from development of the productive forces internationally. Thus it could only expand extensively by utilising vast reservoirs of labour and raw materials. By the mid-1970s and with the end of post-war reconstruction, this avenue was exhausted. A severe economic crisis was almost inevitable as growth rates began to decline.

Only a genuine Communist Party could even attempt a socialist resolution to this crisis. But the Soviet Party had long ceased to represent the working class. The Russian working class, which had accumulated enormous political experience during 1917-1920 was decimated during the Civil War and wars of intervention. The Bolshevik Party lost its best cadres. This set the basis for the decline of the party. Thousands of careerists and anti-socialists joined it to advance their own interests. They initiated the process whereby the Soviet Communist Party was transformed into a vehicle for the accumulation of privilege. Thus grew the *nomenklatura*, a privileged stratum of party officials, state and industrial managers and scientific and cultural workers. Their influence was never to be rooted out. Throughout the post-war period they grew in influence. In all the major social and economic debates they advanced their own interests, separate to those of the working class. Central to all their demands was the restoration of the market.

Gorbachev's accession to power enormously facilitated the advance of the anti-socialists within the Communist Party and the Soviet political establishment. The Soviet economy was showing serious signs of strain. By 1979, GNP per capita in the USSR was only $4,110, compared to $10,630 in the USA. Economic problems, already sub-stantial, were massively aggravated by the imperialist imposed arms race diverting huge resources away from the domestic production. The reactionaries thus seized the initiative, insistently demanding 'market reforms'. To the ailing Soviet economy they contrasted, as models, the 'successful' market economies of Korea and Taiwan. Internationally these trends were encouraged by the advance of the Reagan/Thatcher counter-revolution and the speculative boom in the major capitalist

11

countries. In the absence of any significant communist or Marxist forces within the USSR, Gorbachev's policy of *glasnost* and *perestroika* opened the floodgates for the pro-capitalist elements. The counter-revolutionary forces were ready for their decisive moves.

Nevertheless, despite the Yeltsin August 1991 counter-coup and counter-revolution, capitalist restoration will not be an easy and rapid process. Seventy years of socialist construction has created a massive working class in what was the USSR. This working class is imbued with a collective consciousness and a profound mistrust for free enterprise, private property, the market and capitalism. If the working class succeeds in organising itself as an independent force, the counter-revolution will hit unexpected problems.

Socialism or barbarism

Today bourgeois pundits and ex-Marxists seek to persuade us that the collapse of the socialist bloc irrefutably demonstrated the superiority of capitalism to socialism; that capitalism, not socialism, is best able to meet basic human needs and demands. Such a view can never be accepted by the majority of the world's population. Capitalism has indeed created the material conditions and the productive capacity to house, feed, clothe, educate and cure the world's population. But these have not been put to the service of humanity. Instead, in its relentless and unceasing search for profit – the very essence of the market/capitalist economy – it has subjected the majority of the world's population to unimaginable barbarism.

— Every year 14 million children under the age of five die for lack of medical care;
— 1.5 billion people have no access to any medical care;
— 2 billion people have no permanent water supply;
— 1 billion people live in absolute poverty.

In Latin America 62 per cent of the population, that is 270 million people, live in poverty; 84 million are destitute. There are between 20 and 30 million homeless children on the continent. 30 to 40 per cent of the workforce is either unemployed or underemployed. The World Health Organisation estimates that in the coming period one quarter of Latin Americans – 90-120 million people – could be infected with cholera.

In Africa 27 million people face starvation, in addition to 30 million children afflicted by malnutrition. 150 million people lack safe drinking water and three out of five people have no access to a health service. Annually nearly 150,000 women die during childbirth. Entire countries, such as Liberia and Somalia, are literally disintegrating as a result of imperialist strangulation.

We could travel through Asia and witness similar conditions on a continent where 50 per cent of the population live in poverty. In India 45 million children are wage slaves toiling in conditions more appalling than those of Britain's industrial revolution. In Thailand poverty forces hundreds of thousands of women, young boys and girls into prostitution to cater for imperialist degeneracy. In the Philippines, tens of thousands of families live off rubbish heaps scavenging for salvageable material to sell for the price of a meal.

In contrast to the devastation that free-enterprise and capitalism wrought, attempts to develop a planned economy in what were effectively Third World countries achieved massive advances for the working class and peasantry. As Mark Tully, a BBC correspondent aptly commented when comparing China to India:

'...the fact is that communism has provided better education, better health services and more food and clothes than democracy.'

The argument can be extended. Today, Cuba stands witness to the potential and possibilities of socialism. The advances socialist Cuba has registered for its people are in stark contrast to the deepening poverty and desperation of the masses in Latin America. Despite acute economic crisis following the collapse of the socialist bloc and the tightened vice of US economic and political, blockade, Cuba is making valiant efforts to overcome its severe difficulties in the interests of the majority, the working class and peasantry.

As for the imperialist countries – of course there are those gorged on privilege and luxury. But, as ex-Ugandan President Mr Binasia, now a solicitor for New York City Council, put it: one does not have to go to the Third World to see Third World conditions. One just has to travel to the Bronx. The April/May uprisings in Los Angeles revealed the depth of racism, poverty and destitution in US inner cities. Massive poverty, racist discrimination, rising illiteracy, pollution and industrial and social decay afflict the so-called advanced countries.

These conditions are now being reproduced in the ex-socialist bloc. The processes at work there are summed up by a Hungarian socialist:

'They promised to create a way of life akin to Austria, Germany or Sweden; and they did that – for five per cent of the population. For the rest it is many times worse than British Thatcherism.'

Poverty, hunger, destitution, rabid chauvinism, racism and bloody warfare begin to stalk the once-socialist bloc. Social welfare, education, culture, literature, all the achievements of socialist construction are being destroyed. Meanwhile a tiny minority, in alliance with international capital, is growing wealthy on speculation, robbery, theft and prostitution. The benefits socialism secured, despite enormous difficulties and weaknesses, will not be forgotten. As the logic of the market imposes social, economic and cultural decay and degradation, those taking up the struggle against oppression and exploitation will turn to the history of the socialist bloc for lessons in their own struggle.

Imperialism promises to inflict further horror and barbarism upon the world. For as long as capitalism and imperialism exists the nightmare it has created for humanity will only grow worse. It is no surprise that imperialism is today doubly determined to destroy the remaining socialist countries. They stand as testimony to socialism's capacity to feed, clothe, house and educate the masses, while imperialism only forces them into greater destitution.

The deepening international capitalist crisis promises more social and political instability, more war, suffering, death and destruction. The major imperialist powers are rapidly dividing into hostile blocks as they seek to carve out exclusive spheres of influence as protection against rival capitals. The Japanese and German ruling classes are rewriting their constitutions to launch a new armaments build-up with which to challenge the US's international position. Thus are the major imperialist powers preparing the ground for a new struggle to redivide the world among themselves according to their relative economic strengths. Today's economic warfare promises to turn into tomorrow's carnage and destruction.

Imperialism and capitalism cannot offer peace, stability and progress. To humanity it offers only barbarism, only the bleak prospect of continuing and growing violence, poverty and death. Confronted by such conditions, the working class and oppressed of the world have no choice but to continue the class struggle. The impulse to liberation, to emancipation from the shackles of imperialism and capitalism, from the vice of oppression and exploitation is a fundamental ambition and dream of the exploited and oppressed. This dream cannot be destroyed by the setbacks of the past years. And in the realisation of this dream, the lessons of developments in the ex-socialist bloc and the legacy of Bolshevism will play a central role. They need to be defended and preserved.

EDDIE ABRAHAMS
26 MAY 1992

PART ONE

The Communist heritage

1.1 LEGACY OF THE BOLSHEVIK REVOLUTION
EDDIE ABRAHAMS & MAXINE WILLIAMS
FRFI 103 · OCTOBER/NOVEMBER 1991

The Russian Revolution of 1917, born amid the hope of millions, has finally collapsed. That this colossal and noble effort consciously to seize and control human destiny should have lasted 74 years in the beleaguered Soviet Union is almost miraculous. In the entire history of humanity, it was the first sustained attempt to create a society in the interests of the majority rather than a dominant minority class.

This fragile vessel, the world's first socialist state, navigated uncharted waters amidst a host of dangers. It was holed many times, its timbers became rotten and finally it succumbed to attack from within and without. But not before it had transformed the lives of millions of its own citizens and given substance to the aspirations of billions more throughout the world.

The imperialists greeted the counter-revolution in the Soviet Union with ecstasy. They always feared, loathed and waged war against Soviet power. In unrelenting propaganda they equated communism with tyranny, the destruction of civilisation and the denial of individual human nature. They tried to bury the revolution in this dungheap of abuse precisely because of the simple and terrifying truth it proclaimed – the poor, the majority, can take power from their oppressors.

From day one of the revolution, when they heard that workers and peasants had taken charge, that foreign debts had been cancelled, that the property of their rich Russian cousins had been confiscated, the capitalists declared war. It began with the 1918 invasion by no less than 14 capitalist powers, with Britain at the head. That war has never ceased.

But their current, grotesque dance upon the grave of the revolution is quite futile. The grave contains only old bones. Its flesh and blood, its life and spirit, have long since passed to other parts of the world. There, the oppressed know only too well that capitalism, far from representing the pinnacle of human civilization, represents poverty, dead children, hungry bellies and murdered freedom fighters. They have heard the message that once heard is never forgotten – poor people can take power. That is the gift that the Bolsheviks bequeathed to history. They tried against all odds, to give life to the most liberating and noble ambitions of humanity.

Communism and human liberation

'Philosophers have only interpreted the world, the point however is to change it.'   KARL MARX

Every age has produced thinkers who have fashioned ideas to free humanity from material and spiritual poverty, unleashing its creative potential. In some periods they re-mained isolated thinkers and dream-ers. But in others, periods of turbu-lent social change, those ideas were taken up by vast masses of people and used to shape new institutions. Voltaire, Rousseau and others saw their ideas emblazoned on the ban-ners of the French Revolution as 'liberty, equality and fraternity'. When that revolution had con-solidated the rule of the capitalist class, such dangerous ideas ceased to

VI LENIN

17

have any appeal to the rich and privileged. Henceforth they would devote themselves to the protection of their riches and their philosophers would be paid to pronounce only that we lived in the best of all possible worlds.

From the mid-19th century the task of pushing forward the ideas of progress fell to quite different forces. Marx and Engels forged the communist outlook durng the youth of the working class. This class produced by the capitalist system:

> 'is driven directly to revolt against this inhumanity [of capitalism] . . . The proletariat can and must emancipate itself. But it cannot emancipate itself without abolishing the conditions of its own life. It cannot abolish the conditions of its own life without abolishing all the inhuman conditions of life of society today which are summed up in its own condition.'

Marx and Engels elaborated the fundamental principles of scientific socialism and communism. They proved that capitalism, based on production for profit, could neither fully develop the forces of production nor meet the needs of the majority of humanity. The institutions of the capitalist state, however democratic, expressed only the interests of the minority who owned the means of production. A central condition for emancipation from the horrors of capitalism was proletarian power – the dictatorship of the proletariat. The Paris Commune of 1871 furnished the first brief experience of working class power and the guidelines which inspired the Russian working class of 1917.

The Bolshevik achievement

Perhaps only those alive in 1917 can fully understand the earthquake of the first socialist revolution. Its shockwaves swept the world, a world of war, suffering and starvation. In the trenches, in the stinking slums, in the factories and the streets the thrill was felt. Men and women who previously rotted in the Tsar's gaols were now creating the first socialist state. Soviets, councils of workers and soldiers, were now making the political decisions that previously were the province of a tiny elite.

The Bolshevik programme was Bread, Peace and Land, simple demands that still today represent what two-thirds of human beings in the world lack. This essentially modest programme is precisely what capitalism cannot give them. When the people took power the Russian bourgeoisie resisted with every weapon at its disposal. The majority had spoken but the bourgeoisie, who only talk of democracy to disguise their own dictatorship, resorted to civil war to suppress them. But the lesson of the Commune had been well learned.

'The working class cannot simply lay hold of the old state machinery and wield it for its own purposes.'   KARL MARX

'It must destroy the old capitalist state and use its own organs of power – the people armed – for the forcible suppression of the resistance of the exploiters, ie an insignificant minority of the population, the landowners and the capitalists.'   VI LENIN

It was precisely these measures that the bourgeoisie has always called 'tyranny'. It is not 'tyranny' to starve millions of people, to keep them illiterate, to turn women into chattels, to drive millions into beggary and prostitution. Apparently real 'tyranny' was to execute the Tsar, to divide aristocrats' land among poor peasants, to take the mansions of the rich to house the poor, to forbid the publication of fascist propaganda, to confiscate factories and prohibit individual enrichment through the work of others or speculation.

The achievements of Bolshevik 'tyranny' include: huge strides towards the elimination of poverty, hunger and disease; the education of a previously illiterate population; the survival and cultural advance of nationalities threatened with extinction; the nationalisation of land; and the industrialisation of this vast, backward country through the planned economy.

The torch is passed on

But perhaps the greatest achievement of 1917 came not in the Soviet Union itself but in its international impact. Lenin recognised that capitalism had entered a new stage – of imperialism and parasitic decay.

19

Competing imperialist powers had divided up the world between them, drawing every corner of the globe into their web of exploitation. Henceforth the world was divided into oppressed and oppressor nations. A large section of workers in the imperialist nations had benefited from imperialism and become infected with the diseases of chauvinism and opportunism. The opportunist workers' movements of the imperialist nations had become a major obstacle to the struggle for socialism and against imperialism. The Bolsheviks understood that in this century the torch of revolution would pass to the peoples of the oppressed nations who:

'will participate in deciding the destiny of the whole world and will cease to be simply an object for the enrichment of others.'

Reality has confirmed this. The Russian Revolution swept through the Tsarist Empire to produce the Union of Soviet Socialist Republics. The revolutionary torch passed to Germany, whose workers' revolution was only defeated in blood in 1919, with the complicity of the opportunist Social Democrats. The impulse towards socialism may have begun in Europe but it moved inexorably elsewhere. It is no accident that after 1917 the most authentic socialist revolutions took place in China, Vietnam, Korea and Cuba. The existence of the Soviet Union, its material aid and political support, has been a major factor in allowing these revolutions to survive for so long in the face of such enormous imperialist opposition.

Communism was an international force for democracy. In the 1930s as the threat of fascism grew, the progressive forces of Europe, led by communists, turned to the defence of the Spanish Republic. Huge anti-fascist and resistance movements were formed and, with the prolonged sacrifices of the Soviet people, laid the basis for the defeat of Nazism.

In the post-war period communists stood on the verge of power in Greece and were a serious threat in other European countries. In the wake of liberation by the Red Army and national resistance movements, socialist governments were established in the GDR, Czechoslovakia, Poland, Hungary, Yugoslavia, Albania, Rumania and Bulgaria. The peoples of Asia, Africa and the Arab world continued their resistance to colonialism. Communist North Korea was established in 1948, China in 1949 and North Vietnam in 1954. In 1959 socialist Cuba was established and, with Vietnam, provided the focus for imperialist aggression which continues today. The post-war period saw the overthrow of colonial regimes in most of Africa, Asia and the Middle East. The 1970s witnessed the establishment of revolutionary regimes in Grenada, Nicaragua and Afghanistan. And these are just some, by no means all, of the changes which came in the wake of, and drew strength from, 1917. As Marx once said, 'Well grubbed old Mole'.

Only the first steps

The current round of setbacks, defeats and surrenders may tempt some to say that the old Mole is dead. They are quite wrong. Imperialism has plunged much of the world into terrible poverty. The people of the oppressed nations simply cannot survive in the existing international order. And in the imperialist countries a growing number of people live in poverty, insecurity, pollution and cultural privation. The imperialist countries are armed to the teeth and limbering up through economic competition for redividing the world. There is no peace, progress or security in the new world order. It is as inevitable as day following night that socialism will revive anew.

And it is thanks to the efforts, sacrifices and hard-won lessons of the Bolsheviks and the revolutions which have followed, that the next round of the socialist revolution will begin from an incomparably higher stage. Future socialist efforts will not blindly follow the Soviet model. Its gains, and there were many, were made in the most difficult of circumstances (including a war in which 25 million Soviet citizens died) and against the most concerted imper-

STORMING THE WINTER PALACE, 1917

ialist opposition. These pressures exhausted the revolution. The leaders and masses alike were drained, and lost their connection with each other. The impetus dwindled and development became ossification; timeserving careerists replaced revolutionaries; sacrifice became privilege; communism lapsed into social democracy.

But as Marx said of the Commune:

'The working class did not expect miracles from the Commune. They have no ready-made utopias to introduce *par decret du peuple*. They know that in order to work out their emancipation, and along with it that higher form to which present society is tending by its own economical agencies, they will have to pass through long struggles, through a series of historic processes, transforming circumstances and men.'

The twentieth century has been the century of first steps in this 'historic process'. There is much for socialists now to learn from the successes and failures, the tragedies and sacrifices. There is an indescribably rich tradition which this international effort has left us. All the revolutions and uprisings adapted their programmes to suit their conditions and fought to produce solutions to immensely varied problems. But all took their inspiration from 1917. It is now the task of communists every-where to study those lessons and absorb the contributions of nearly a century of international effort before we can go forward again. ∎

1.2 IN DEFENCE OF LENIN
ANDY HIGGINBOTTOM
FRFI 99 · FEBRUARY/MARCH 1991

Lenin brought communism into the 20th century. Leader of the Bolshevik Party and the Russian proletariat, inspiration of the first-ever successful socialist revolution in October 1917 and of the Communist International, Lenin's contribution to the cause of the working class and oppressed is immense. But social democratic ideologues are determined to destroy every vestige of Leninist influence.

In 1990, a stream of 'Marxists' were promoted to near celebrity status in the bourgeois media. Their brief was not to praise Lenin, but to bury him:

'Lenin, the man, died in 1924. But Lenin, the icon of Soviet power, is meeting its end today . . . Thanks to the revolutions of Eastern Europe, time has run out for Lenin.'
ORLANDO FIGES, THE GUARDIAN 30 APRIL 1990

It is not enough for the imperialist powers that socialism has collapsed in Eastern Europe. Imperialism seeks to eradicate the very idea that socialism is possible. In fact it is the opponents of revolution who reduce Lenin to an icon rather than address the substance of his ideas. Why? Because of their potency and relevance. Lenin's political thought culminates in his analysis of imperialism and the necessity of an actual struggle for socialism.

Imperialism and the split in socialism

In 1916 Lenin showed that the concentration of production in the hands of a few massive capitalist associations, fusion of banking with industrial capital, the export of capital to set up production with cheap labour in the oppressed nations, and competition between the major capitalist nations to grab each other's colonial possessions were features which together defined a qualitatively new era. Imperialism, Lenin argued, was both the highest and the last stage of capitalism (*Collected Works* (CW), Vol 22, p266).

With the onset of worldwide imperialism what had been a specific feature of England's colonial monopoly in the 19th century, the exploitation of oppressed nations and the creation of a labour aristocracy which 'lives partly at the expense of hundreds of millions in the uncivilised nations', becomes the central issue for all political class struggle (CW, Vol 23, p107). Lenin re-established the communist tradition founded on Marx and Engels' fight against opportunism in the English labour movement.

For Lenin, imperialism was not only a matter of economics. He

23

sought in economics the material basis of and explanation for the shocking betrayal in 1914, when nine-tenths of the leaders of the Second International supported their own 'fatherland' in killing workers from other countries.

'Opportunism means sacrificing the fundamental interests of the masses to the temporary interests of an insignificant minority of the workers . . . an alliance between a section of the workers and the bourgeoisie . . . Opportunism was engendered in the course of decades by the special features in the period of development of capitalism, when the comparatively peaceful and cultured life of a stratum of working men "bourgeoisified" them, gave them crumbs from the table of their national capitalists, and isolated them from the suffering, misery and revolutionary temper of the impoverished and ruined masses.' CW, VOL 21, pp242-3

Lenin saw the need to break the working class from the influence of opportunism represented by two political trends which appeared inevitably in all the imperialist countries. The first trend, of bourgeois labour parties, rejected the class struggle, promoted national chauvinism and openly collaborated with their own governments. The second trend, of opportunism, was represented by Karl Kautsky, the leading theoretician of the Second International. Kautsky, while continuing to use the language of Marxism, opposed the war in words but accepted it in deeds. The epitome of Kautsky's opportunism was his refusal to take advantage of the crisis, seize the initiative and turn the imperialist war into a civil war.

The workers' revolution of October 1917 would not have been possible without the prolonged struggle by Lenin to defeat these opportunist trends internationally and in Russia. This was Lenin's own assessment:

'One of the principle reasons why Bolshevism was able to achieve victory in 1917-20 was that, since the end of 1914, it has been ruthlessly exposing the baseness and vileness of social-chauvinism and "Kautskyism" (to which . . . the views of the Fabians and the leaders of the Independent Labour Party in Britain . . . correspond),

the masses later becoming more and more convinced, from their
own experience, of the correctness of the Bolshevik views.'
CW, VOL 31, p29

For Lenin the ·masses had to be brought into politics, and their
'revolutionary temper' realised as the decisive factor. Early in 1917 the
Russian proletarians rediscovered their own invention, the Soviets,
councils of action embracing the masses of workers, soldiers and
peasantry. From April onwards Lenin argued for all power to the
Soviets, for an insurrection, for the dictatorship of the proletariat, for
socialist revolution.

Not surprisingly it was Kautsky who immediately after the Russian
revolution became the 'principal theoretical antagonist of Bolshevism'.
He played a counter-revolutionary role in stopping the German
proletariat, 'from following the revolutionary road opened up by the
Russian working class'.

The split in the socialist movement between communism and social
democracy was irrevocable. The Russian Bolsheviks formed the Third
Communist International. Lenin told delegates at its first major
congress that an essential condition of the Bolsheviks' revolutionary
success had been 'the most rigorous and truly iron discipline in our
Party', and urged the formation of like parties as the most conscious
political expression of the proletariat (CW, Vol 31, pp23-26).

The Communist Party in Britain was thus ostensibly conceived in
order to fight imperialism and combat opportunism in the working
class. It has since turned into the opposite, and become an agent of a
latter day, pro-imperialist, Kautskyism.

End of the road for the British Communist Party

The retreat of socialism in 1989/90 has pushed Communist Parties
across the world onto the defensive. British CP leader Chris Myant does
not attempt to defend socialism. He seizes on the problems of the
socialist countries to disavow the communist tradition:

'The time has come when it is now possible for communists to face a very difficult truth. October 1917, the world event which separates communists from others on the left, was a mistake of truly historic proportions.

Its consequences have been severe. They have characterised and moulded the great traumas of the 20th century: a second world war; Hitler's gas chambers; Stalin's gulag; the world of the show trials; the perpetuation of Third World fascist dictatorships; the unprecedented, almost unbelievable waste of the arms race in a world of poverty and starvation; the destruction of the Vietnam war ...' SEVEN DAYS, 24 FEBRUARY 1990

How debased can you get? The Bolsheviks who dared to take power and strove to build a new world have somehow become responsible for imperialism's crimes against humanity.

Myant tries to set an isolated 'dictatorial' Lenin against the 'democratic' mainstream of scientific socialism:

'When they first wrote the *Communist Manifesto* in 1848 Marx and Engels were thinking of a sudden dramatic break between capitalism and the future society of socialism, of a revolution in which the institutions of the old order were "smashed" ... At the end of his life Engels rejected his 1848 analysis ... It was against the ideas of building upon so-called bourgeois democracy, ideas that flowed from Engels' rejection of the concept of "overthrow", that Lenin spent virtually all his life polemicising.'

Marx and Engels *did* change their position on the state, but it was in the *opposite* direction to that which Myant claims. Lenin's *The State and Revolution*, published in August 1917 in order to '*re-establish* what Marx really taught on the subject of the state', explains with exceptional clarity that Marx and Engels learnt from the European revolutions of 1848-51, and especially from the experience of the Paris Commune, that is after they had written the *Communist Manifesto*.

The dictatorship of the proletariat

In 1871 French workers 'stormed the gates of heaven'. For two months Paris was under elective workers control, then the bourgeoisie regained the upper hand and drowned the first workers' revolution in blood. In their 1872 Preface to the *Manifesto* Marx and Engels stressed that its programme of revolutionary measures, 'has in some details become antiquated', and that:

> 'One thing especially was proved by the Commune, *viz.*, that "the working class cannot simply lay hold of the ready-made state machinery, and wield it for its own purposes" '.
>
> CW, VOL 25, p385

It was Marx and Engels who increasingly emphasised that the capitalist state would have to be 'smashed'. The capitalist class is the ruling class by virtue of its control of the repressive, administrative state apparatus. The state is never neutral, always it is a class power. Capital will not voluntarily give up state power; on the contrary it will use 'special bodies of armed men, prisons etc.' to enforce its rule.

The working class cannot simply 'lay hold' of this apparatus to defend its social and economic interests as a class. It must make a political revolution to abolish the capitalist state. Engels' later historical analyses became 'a veritable panegyric on violent revolution'.

The dictatorship of the proletariat summarises a new type of state, not just a change of government. Whatever the form of government – monarchy, parliamentary democracy, fascist dictatorship – the capitalist state must be overthrown.

The Communist Party is therefore essential. It must direct the most conscious section of the working class, its vanguard which leads the masses in a revolution for state power.

KARL MARX

Lenin addressed the socio-economic basis of the withering away of the state under the proletarian dictatorship. Communist society is organised around production for need, not for profit. The transition to communism is *only possible after the working class has political power*.

Those revisionists of Marxism, like Kautsky in Lenin's time and Myant today, who reject the dictatorship of the proletariat, not only vulgarise the teachings of Marx and Engels, *they reject even the possibility of ever achieving communism*.

For Lenin, for creative Marxism

By the turn of this century capitalism encompassed the globe. Its potential appeared to be limitless. The better-off Western European workers were being drawn into government. It seemed that the working class majority could be transformed into a parliamentary majority which would harness social production for the common good. The Fabians in Britain and Edward Bernstein in Germany argued that Marxism was old-fashioned, confined to the growing pains of capitalism in the 19th century. They even adopted a 'socialist colonial policy'.

Then the storm broke. The horrors of the First World War brought home to European workers what the peoples colonised by imperialist expansion had never been allowed to forget, the bloody barbarism of the capitalist system.

In this last decade of the 20th century we are reliving the themes with which it began. Marxism has come under attack for similar reasons, apparent stability provided by another 'New World Order'. Myant finds much to commend in the 'advanced industrial states', and, 'the richness and depth of the civil society and political plurality that has grown up in these societies'. This Eurocentric, and ultimately racist, celebration of the vitality of bourgeois democracy is only possible for someone who has enjoyed the benefits of a welfare state while the rest of the world is starving. Myant, like Kautsky and Bernstein before him, spoke too soon. Imperialism has once again plunged the world into crisis and war.

Lenin's great political courage in transforming the carnage of war into the first socialist revolution charted the way forward for his generation and ours. The Soviet Revolution forged a bridgehead of hope into the future. Marx and Engels understood that in creating the working class, capitalism creates the force that will become its own gravedigger. Lenin applied this insight to modern conditions. Imperialism has created its own gravediggers in the thousands of millions in the oppressed nations. The proletarian dictatorship must inevitably assume different forms. Lenin pointed to this potential diversity in his prophetic *Our Revolution*:

'Our European philistines never even dream that the subsequent revolutions in Oriental countries, which. possess much vaster populations and a much vaster diversity of social conditions, will undoubtedly display even greater distinctions than the Russian revolution.'   CW, VOL 33, p480

The shift in the locus of communism to oppressed nations is no accident of history, but a consequence of resistance movements which put revolutionary theories to the test of practice.

The fundamental division of the world between oppressor and oppressed nations is mirrored by the division of socialism within the working class of the oppressor nations. The conclusion of the Leninist analysis is the imperative necessity for communists to combat the pro-imperialist trends in the working class. Workers in the oppressor nations must support the oppressed in order to weaken their common enemy and bring about the socialist revolution. Leninist anti-imperialism is the starting point for the formation of a Communist Party in Britain today.   ■

FREDERICK ENGELS

1.3 MARXISM, THE RUSSIAN REVOLUTION AND THE 'NEW LEFT'
EDDIE ABRAHAMS
FRFI 106 · APRIL/MAY 1992

The collapse of the socialist bloc has given a field day to 'left-wing' critics of Marxism-Leninism. Among them is Robin Blackburn, editor of *New Left Review* (NLR). His article 'Fin de siècle: Socialism after the Crash', published in NLR 185, aims to drive a wedge between socialism and Marxism-Leninism. In opposition to the Third International's communist traditions, Blackburn works to rehabilitate the standpoint of Second International social democracy.

Blackburn was once a defender of Leninism. Today, his transformation into a social democrat mirrors the fate of a substantial section of middle class socialists who constituted the 'revolutionary left' of the 1960s and 1970s. Then they adopted revolutionary, even Marxist, phrases. But as a social group their aim was only to frighten existing authority for a greater share of material privilege. Today they no longer need Marxism. Marxism is not compatible with the defence of privilege. So instead they turn to left-social democracy. The collapse of the socialist bloc provides their excuse to settle accounts with their 'revolutionary' ideals.

Blackburn opens by telling us that:

'the ruin of "Marxism-Leninism" has been sufficiently comprehensive to eliminate it as an alternative to capitalism and compromise the very idea of socialism.'

He then sets out to account for 'the dire experience of communism since 1917'.

What is this 'dire experience'? The free social and medical provision and guaranteed employment provided to the ex-Soviet people? Soviet support for national liberation movements? Support for Cuba? Can anti-fascist veterans of World War II believe communism since 1917 was a 'dire experience'?

Clearly Blackburn examines the Soviet experience from the standpoint of the materially comfortable middle class of the imperialist countries. A communist examines the problems and failings of communism since 1917 within the context of its fundamentally progressive role. Social democrats regard the socialist bloc's irrefutably positive features as incidental elements of a fundamentally 'dire experience'.

Blackburn, Marxism and Leninism

Having thus dismissed communism, Blackburn turns on those he deems responsible – Lenin and the Bolshevik Party:

> 'With respect to mainstream Marxism, Lenin's Bolshevik current came to represent a species of political voluntarism.'

By this Blackburn means that in 1917 the Bolsheviks acted without regard for objective economic and social conditions and attempted a premature revolution. To sustain this case he rehabilitates, as 'notable Marxists of the day', Second International theoreticians such as Kautsky, Plekhanov and Martov who broke with Marxism in 1914! In the 20th century the socialist movement's standpoint on imperialism, war, national liberation and socialist revolution – right up to the dictatorship of the proletariat – defines the divide between communists and social democrats, between revolutionaries and opportunists. On all these issues, Kautsky and Co adopted a reactionary stand.

After 1914 the international socialist movement – the Second International – split over these issues. During the first 1914-1918 Imperialist War for the redistribution of the oppressed nations among the imperialist powers, Kautsky and Co refused to oppose the warmongering of their own imperialist ruling class. After the war and its resulting carnage and hunger, revolutions shook the foundations of the capitalist order in Europe. In all cases Blackburn's 'notable Marxists' opposed these revolutions and opposed the the dictatorship of the proletariat – the transfer of political power to the working class.

The Third, Communist, International emerged to fight the treachery of the Second International. Within it, Marxist-Leninists were in fact 'the mainstream'. They recognised the 1914-1918 war as imperialist and, unlike Kautsky and Co, called for self-determination for oppressed nations. They also urged the working class to transform the war into a civil war and socialist revolution. Ignoring these fundamental divisions, Blackburn invokes Kautsky's authority to condemn Lenin and the Bolshevik Party as a 'conspiratorial, Jacobin, doctrinaire strain' within socialism! Such epithets only disguise opposition to the overthrow of capitalism and the dictatorship of the proletariat. For social democracy discussion of revolution is always 'doctrinaire', the seizure of political power by the working class 'political voluntarism' and the dictatorship of the proletariat a 'Jacobin excess'.

Blackburn also dishonestly uses Trotsky and Rosa Luxemburg against Lenin, claiming they criticised his theory of the party 'for its Jacobinism and commandism'. True, Trotsky did so, but later, after conceding he had been wrong, he joined the Bolshevik Party in 1917 and played a leading role in the Revolution. Rosa Luxemburg also had many criticisms of the Bolshevik Party. But her overall assessment was that:

> 'All the revolutionary honour and capacity which western social democracy lacked were represented by the Bolsheviks. Their October uprising was not only the actual salvation of the Russian Revolution; it was also the salvation of the honour of international socialism.'

Blackburn and the Russian Revolution

Blackburn, in contrast, believes the Russian Revolution to have been an historic error. He quotes Kautsky:

> 'The Bolsheviks . . . tackled problems for the solution of which all conditions were lacking.'

And adds that:

> 'Kautsky pointed out that they lacked the requisite social basis and capacity for true socialisation and sustained, diversified economic growth.'

This is the Second International, Menshevik, refrain. Russia was economically backward, capitalism was underdeveloped and the working class a minority. A socialist revolution, therefore, would be premature; its objective basis – developed capitalism – did not exist. The working class, in consequence, must limit its struggle to attaining a bourgeois democratic republic. Anything more would be 'political voluntarism'.

In fact, the Bolsheviks were aware of the immense problems posed by Russian economic and cultural backwardness. But they saw Russia as the 'weak link' in a system of imperialist/capitalist states and the revolution as part of an international socialist offensive, taking in the more advanced capitalist countries. Lenin noted:

'Regarded from the world-historical point of view, there would doubtlessly be no hope for the ultimate victory of our revolution, if we were to remain alone.'

He insisted that:

'... our salvation ... is an all European revolution.'

After the 1914-1918 war, revolutions did sweep across Europe – Germany, Italy, Austria and Hungary. In all cases they were suppressed, with utmost savagery, by Second International 'socialists' in alliance with the ruling class. German social democracy even murdered Rosa Luxemburg and Karl Liebknecht!

Given the historical circumstances the Bolshevik Party did the only thing possible. A revolution does not involve only individuals, parties or single classes. It is a massive explosion of social, economic and political contradictions which cannot be contained within the old regime. It is an acute sharpening of class antagonisms to the point of insurrection and civil war. In such situations compromise is not possible. One or the other main class, in alliance with sections of other classes, must prevail and impose its will on society.

Such was the Russian Revolution. The old Tsarist ruling class was an alliance of landed aristocrats and the industrial bourgeoisie backed by a fascist military clique led by Kornilov (the Russian Pinochet, Shah or Somosa). Against it stood the millions of peasants and workers driven to revolt by the intolerable conditions of war and famine. A bourgeois social democratic republic in Russia, devastated by war and with no imperialist plunder, was the pipe dream of Plekhanov and the Mensheviks.

Had the Russian working class not seized power and ruthlessly suppressed the White Counter-Revolution, the Russian ruling class would have imposed a military tyranny and crushed all the democratic and social aspirations of the working class and peasantry. The truth of this was proven in regions captured by the Whites during the Civil War.

History has confirmed the Bolshevik position. The Revolution, burdened by massive economic backwardness, was subjected to relentless imperialist encirclement, military assault and economic sabotage. As a result it suffered enormous defects and weaknesses. Nevertheless, the Soviet economy, on the basis of incredibly small resources, began to systematically eliminate poverty, illiteracy, hunger and homelessness and secured enormous cultural advances for the masses.

Rather than attribute the Revolution's failings to the 'Jacobin' or 'voluntarist' 'excesses' of Leninism, we adopt Rosa Luxemburg's Marxist approach:

> 'The blame for the failures of Bolshevism is borne in the final analysis by the international proletariat and above all by the unprecedented and persistent baseness of German [we would add – British] social democracy.'

Blackburn, Marx and the market

Having rehabilitated the Second International to attack Leninism, Blackburn turns to attack the socialist planned economy. In defence of his alternative 'socialised market', he rehabilitates, among others, Marx's anarchist critics! After all some of Marx's 'rhetoric now seems overly simple'. Marxism also contains a 'strain of . . . arrogance towards small producers'. In contrast Proudhon, 'acclaimed a precursor of market socialism', 'had a greater sensitivity . . . to the significance of petty production and exchange'. Bakunin, 'who was worried that Marx had too narrow a conception of who was a worker', had 'prescient remarks' on the dangers of 'state socialism'.

Having thus enriched his thought, Blackburn advances a strikingly new 'starting point for politics and economics' – not the class interests of the working class, not the emancipation of humanity from the shackles of capital. No. The starting point 'must be' . . . 'respect for individual choice'! And the market is the best mechanism! The market:

'. . . in and through the reactions to it also broadens the potential scope of human solidarity.'

Go and tell that to the starving people in the African continent's market, to the street children in Brazil's market, to the impoverished millions in the ex-USSR's newly installed market!

For Blackburn the market is a neutral mechanism, even 'an aspect of the forces of production' amenable to socialist regulation. In fact, in the real world, the market is far from a neutral, technical factor of economic production. It expresses a social relation of capitalist production. Under capitalism, production and distribution, carried out individually, for profit not for social use, are regulated unconsciously by the law of value which acquires social form in the market. The market, by its mere existence, expresses the anarchy of production – the fact that society does not control production and cannot consciously organise it towards desired social ends.

The economic plan, on the other hand, expresses social relations of production which are organised and regulated consciously by society in the interests of society. The central-ised economic plan is the socialist method of overcoming the isolated individual capitalist production, of overcoming the anarchy and waste of capitalist production.

The market and the plan are not compatible. They each express

'RUN OVER YELTSIN WITH A TRAIN!'

different class interests. A socialist state may be forced to rely on severely limited market mechanisms – but only as a temporary measure. Eventually one or the other, the market or the plan, the bourgeoisie or the working class must prevail.

Blackburn's theory is so much cosmetic to disguise a rehash of the discredited Left Alternative Strategy of the 1970s. In place of a centrally planned economy, he offers a fantasy – a combination of market and plan, a regulated market which curbs capitalist exploitation without abolishing capital. Wishing to achieve 'socialism' without revolution and class struggle, he devises a 'system' which satisfies all classes – workers, bankers, petty producers, entrepreneurs and even the ecologically-concerned street traders.

Through 'taxation and social insurance' a progressive government 'could prevent class-like inequalities' resulting from the market. Private capital would become a 'socialist entrepreneuralism' without the 'momentum of capitalist accumulation and its propensity to plunder and divide'. And tax breaks would restore morality to banks and holding companies by 'encouraging' them to offer funds for 'socially desirable investments'. The central planning authorities in a 'socialised market' 'could also devise effective but socially less disruptive and painful substitutes for bankruptcy and unemployment.'

Imperialist capital, without a qualm, murders hundreds of thousands for the sake of profit. It will not sit idly by and allow Blackburn's 'socialist authorities' to curb its appetites. Capital's urge for profit, its relentless creation of inequality, its total disregard for 'socially desirable investment' can only be destroyed by suppressing the capitalist class, by establishing working class political power – the dictatorship of the proletariat. It can only be eventually destroyed by the systematic development of the planned economy and the total overcoming of the market.

Yet Blackburn rejects these measures and the legacy of Leninism and the Russian Revolution. In doing so he rejects the first significant lessons for a genuine transition from capitalist barbarism to socialism.■

1.4 THE MARKET VERSUS THE PLAN: CHE GUEVARA'S HERITAGE
EDDIE ABRAHAMS
FRFI 90 · OCTOBER 1989

Carlos Tablada's *Che Guevara: Economics and Politics in the Transition to Socialism* (Pathfinder Press, 1989) is a splendid polemic against the petit bourgeois notion of 'market socialism' now gaining ascendancy in many socialist countries and among opportunists in imperialist nations.

Between 1963 and 1965, Cuban communists conducted a major debate on the problems confronting the Cuban economy. Che Guevara, then Minister of Industry, made enormous theoretical and political contributions to this debate. Through a detailed examination of these, Tablada demonstrates that the resort to 'market socialism' – the law of value, market forces, competition, material incentives and private enterprise – to overcome economic crises in socialist countries threatens the very foundations of socialism itself.

Against the 'market socialists' of his day Che conducted a vigorous ideological and political battle. He sought:

'. . . socialist formulas rather than capitalist formulas to solve problems, because before we realise it capitalist formulas can begin to corrupt us and contaminate us.'

During the debates he developed a superb defence of Marxism ('that towering doctrine') and of Marx's *Capital* ('a monument of the human mind'). Together, Che's contributions constitute a solid foundation for a communist standpoint on the transition to socialism.

Planned economy – a foundation of socialism

Most socialist countries are today resorting to market mechanisms hoping these will boost production where the centralised planned economy failed. In tandem petit bourgeois revisionists, many inside socialist countries, are calling into question the very necessity and even the feasibility of a centralised and planned economy to build socialism.

A dominant theme of this book is its defence of the planned economy against those singing loud and gaudy praises to the capitalist market. Tablada correctly argues that in the anti-capitalist revolution, the dictatorship of the proletariat and the planned economy are inseparably linked. The planned economy is the only means by which humanity can overcome the anarchy of capitalism. It is the only way that humanity, instead of being subjugated by the process of production, can acquire mastery over it and consciously direct it towards socially desired ends. It is therefore the only way in which the immense majority of humanity can overthrow the terrible burden of exploitation, oppression, poverty, hunger, and misery which is its lot under capitalism. As Che put it:

'... centralised planning is the mode of existence of socialist society, its defining characteristic and the point at which man's consciousness finally succeeds in synthesising and directing the economy towards its goal: the full liberation of the human being in the context of communist society.'

Che rejected the use of market mechanisms because they undermine the planned economy and give greater freedom for the operation of the capitalist law of value. As a result, they facilitate the development of capitalist tendencies within socialist countries. Proponents of 'market socialism', today triumphant in Poland and Hungary, and spreading rapidly in other socialist countries, were peddling their wares back in the early 1960s. Che had to fight theoreticians from Hungary, Czechoslovakia and the Soviet Union who claimed that the law of value and the market are not uniquely capitalist but have universal validity and can be used within the plan to develop socialism. On the contrary he retorted angrily: 'The law of value and the plan are two terms linked by a contradiction and its resolution.'

The law of value is a historically determined feature of commodity production and finds its fullest expression in the anarchy of the capitalist market, in the exploitation of the working class and the plunder of oppressed nations. It has nothing in common with socialism. The law of value is but the manner in which economic equilibrium is established – spontaneously, unconsciously – in capitalist society. In socialist society, equilibrium is established in the interests of society, by the majority, through the plan – in a conscious and rational manner. Che was not however a dogmatist or an ultra-leftist and recognised that whilst imperialism lasts and socialism is yet in its early stage of development, the law of value would continue to exercise its influence, particularly through the international capitalist market. But, unlike our modern revisionists, he did not see this as a blessing to be multiplied. The law of value was an 'umbilical cord tying the new society to the old' and should be suppressed by the systematic development of the conscious power of the centralised and planned economy.

The Party, the masses and democracy

Che coupled his defence of the planned economy with an insistence that in the period of transition, political and ideological leadership by the working class vanguard organised in the Communist Party remains indispensable. Without such a party, committed to mass democratic participation and guided by the most advanced theory and the highest moral values, the planned economy would fail and socialism would remain in constant danger.

Che rejected the revisionist view that *economic production* could be separated from the *production and reproduction of communist social relations and consciousness*. Whilst the centralised economic plan was an indispensable foundation for socialism, the Communist Party could not reduce its role to the technical and administrative organisation of the economy and material production. 'We cannot arrive at communism through simple mechanical accumulation of quantities of goods', Che wrote, adding that: 'Building socialism . . . combines work and consciousness – expanding the production of material goods through work and developing consciousness.'

CHE GUEVARA

39

The planned economy and socialism would develop sucessfully only if it ran parallel with the development of a new communist social consciousness. However, such a consciousness, while requiring a planned economy as its base, does not flow from it automatically. Developing communist values and principles, developing the 'new communist person', will only flow from the conscious ideological and political work of a communist leadership.

The leading ideological and political role of the Communist Party is particularly necessary given the deeply ingrained petit bourgeois selfishness and individualism we inherit from capitalism and the incredibly difficult objective conditions in which socialism is being built. Success in the combined task of developing the planned economy and creating a new communist consciousness – ie building socialism – requires the vanguard party to work to actively involve the masses in political, social and economic life, for:

> 'Building socialism is based on the work of the masses, on the capacity of the masses to be able to organise themselves to better guide industry, agriculture and the country's economy.'

Only if the Party remains 'in constant and permanent touch with the masses', will it really be capable of representing their interests and leading them. Only in such a relationship with the masses will a communist leadership succeed in coping with the enormous and difficult challenges and problems of building socialism. These elementary lessons need repeating a hundred times in light of the bitter experience of honest communists in Poland, Hungary and other socialist countries. In many cases, Communist Parties having lost any connection with the masses, have become vehicles for pro-capitalist elements eager to resort to 'capitalist formulas'. As a result the socialist planned economy and the development of that new communist consciousness necessary to defend socialism have suffered irreparable harm.

Capitalist mechanisms and communist consciousness

Che Guevara's opposition to the use of 'capitalist formulas' thus took into account not just their adverse effect on the planned economy but also their negative ideological and political effects. In debate against opponents in Cuba and other socialist countries, Che argued that a narrow technical and administrative approach to economic planning put at risk ideological and political factors vital for socialism. Tablada puts the issue very effectively:

'Seeking purely economic gains could lead to the application of methods that produce short term results at the expense of mortgaging the revolution's future through the steady erosion of the process of developing consciousness.'

One example of this is the offer of material incentives to increase production. In the short term this may raise production, but only at the expense of creating a new social consciousness. Che opposed material incentives. The idea of rewarding *individuals* with material incentives to boost production serving *collective* ends was a contradiction. It could only help sustain individual selfishness and greed. Material incentives:

'come from capitalism and are destined to die under socialism. [They] are remnants of the past . . . [and] will play no part in the new society that is being created.'

Che believed that:

'The role of the vanguard party is precisely that of raising as high as possible the opposing banner, the banner of moral interests, of moral incentives . . . '

Che recognised, however, that in Cuba, given the backward economy, there unfortunately remains an objective need for material incentives to ensure effective production. However, he was 'reluctant' to use them and always attempted to offer them in a social not individual form.

The dangers of treating economic production and economic planning as a purely administrative and technical matter were evident to Che. In countries with a backward economy, suffering imperialist encirclement and weighed down by decades of imperialist and capitalist oppression, the temptation for quick economic results easily lends itself to adopting 'capitalist formulas'. But these threaten centralised economic planning, the foundation of socialism, and undermine communist social consciousness. Together, such developments guarantee the survival and growth of pro-capitalist tendencies and ambitions within the socialist countries themselves, presenting long term dangers to their very survival.

It was within these parameters that Che Guevara advanced his many concrete proposals for dealing with Cuba's economic problems. This book sets out, in some detail, Che's Budgetary Finance System for the planned economy, his wage system which takes into account 'facts of consciousness', his views and proposals on money, on voluntary labour, on the necessity for communist party members to have the highest moral standards and principles, on the need for a new international economic order and on the absolute necessity for revolutionary internationalism.

Tablada's merit and great strength is that in exposing 'market socialism' as a theory, he relies not on Che's undoubted revolutionary authority, but on the presentation of his theoretical and political ideas – whose brilliance and profoundness is confirmed by their relevance today. ■

Biographical note:

Che Guevara (1928-1967) was one of the most remarkable leaders to emerge from the Cuban Revolution. Born in Argentina in 1928 he abandoned the possibility of a very privileged life and joined Fidel Castro in the guerrilla struggle against the Batista dictatorship in 1959. In socialist Cuba he served as President of the National Bank and as Minister of Industry. After 1965 he resigned his official positions and went to Bolivia to open a new guerrilla front against imperialism. In 1967 he was captured and murdered by the Bolivian army. His writings, his dedication, his commitment and self-sacrifice continue to inspire all those fighting for socialism.

The most accessible selection of Che's writings is *Che Guevara and the Cuban Revolution: Writings and Speeches of Ernesto Che Guevara* published by Pathfinder Press.

1.5 THE RUSSIAN REVOLUTION AND THE NATIONAL QUESTION
TED TALBOT
FRFI 100 · APRIL/MAY 1991

In December 1922 the First All-Union Congress of Soviets declared the formation of the Union of Soviet Socialist Republics. Such a Union was necessary both to combat the threat of internal counter-revolution and external intervention. They believed that it would have been hard to safeguard Soviet power and the independence of the country, surrounded as it was by militarily strong capitalist powers. This would require uniting to the fullest extent the fraternal Republics' military, political and diplomatic efforts. The vital interests of all the Soviet peoples and the struggle for socialism demanded the formation of a united multinational socialist state.

This illustrates a contradiction for Leninists with their theoretical commitment to self-determination. Revolutions which have created the conditions in which the secession of oppressed nations is possible are liable to be irretrievably weakened if this right is immediately exercised. Furthermore, it is precisely in the midst of revolutionary ferment that an impetus to independence is likely to be strongest. In fact the Bolshevik Party was clear that the right to self-determination was subordinate to the needs of socialist construction.

Let us follow up this notion of discord between theory and practice. For example, the following retort addressed to Polish communists in a debate about the legitimacy of annexations is typical of Lenin's vociferous support for national self-determination.

'However you may twist and turn, annexation is *violation of the self-determination* of a nation, it is the establishment of state *frontiers contrary to the will of the population.*'
VI LENIN 'THE RIGHT OF NATIONS TO SELF-DETERMINATION'

In March 1920 Pilsudski's Polish army invaded Soviet territory and established a base in the raw materials-rich Ukraine for a few months. They were driven out by the Red Army and the Politbureau had to decide whether to pursue the retreating Poles into their own territory. Rejecting Trotsky's advice, Lenin, along with the majority of the

Politbureau, decided to invade Poland for the following reasons:

1. A tactical military reason – Pilsudski was unlikely to accept the territorial frontier demarcated by the Bolsheviks and was likely simply to use the time to regroup his forces.
2. A political reason – they thought that the advance of the Red Army would promote revolutionary outbreaks in Poland.
3. Poland was the bridge between Russia and Germany, and across it Lenin hoped to establish contact with Germany, imagining that Germany, too, was in intense revolutionary ferment.

It is pertinent to note that Trotsky's reservations were based not on matters of principle, but rather on warnings of an upsurge of Polish patriotic sentiment following a Red Army invasion of Poland which he received from Polish socialists in Moscow.

The Polish experience was a watershed not just in Bolshevik practice but also in its contradiction of theoretical propositions. 'It had been a canon of Marxist politics that revolution cannot and must not be carried out on the point of bayonets into foreign countries.' (*The Prophet Armed. Trotsky: 1879-1921*, Isaac Deutscher). In short, in practice Lenin and the Bolsheviks were prepared to view national self-determination as secondary to the interests of socialism.

Today nationalist resurgence is threatening the integrity of the Soviet Union. Ten of the 15 republics are claiming various degrees of autonomy with the Baltic states in the lead. The drive for national autonomy is inextricably intertwined with moves towards a market economy and greater ties with the West.

On Sunday 1 March, two unofficial referenda in Estonia (83 per cent turnout, 78 per cent pro-independence) and Latvia (88 per cent turnout, 83 per cent pro-independence) saw huge majorities in favour of independence, despite the presence of sizeable pro-Moscow organisations which have complained of ballot rigging and intimidation of voters. For instance in Daugavpils in Latvia only 13 per cent of the population is ethnic Latvian, yet even here a 51 per cent vote favouring independence was recorded. A previous straw ballot in Lithuania had produced an extraordinary result of 90 per cent in favour of independence.

It is unlikely that these results will be repeated in the national referendum currently taking place. This asks whether the present national boundaries of the USSR should be maintained. Six republics are refusing to take part in the vote. Gorbachev has warned that a 'no' vote, leading to the break-up of the Soviet Union, would be 'a world disaster'.

The policy of *glasnost* has allowed a multitude of national grievances to enter the public arena. Some of these grievances may be legitimate but the secession of one republic would surely promote what Gorbachev's adviser, Alexander Yakolev, terms a 'domino effect' which would rapidly lead to the dismemberment of the Soviet Union.

It is fairly clear, as much as anything is clear from his contradictory statements, that Gorbachev, whether from personal disposition or due to pressure from the KGB/military etc, is prepared to allow substantial degrees of national autonomy but not to countenance the destruction of the USSR:

> 'Disintegration and separation cannot happen in our country, simply under any circumstances . . . If we start splitting, there will be a dreadful war.'

What should be the attitude of Marxists in this situation? Can the conception that the interests of socalism are superior to the concern for independence apply here also? To accept such a qualification puts one in total opposition to the overwhelming majority of Trotskyist groups (with the exception of the Spartacists), who uncritically support independence moves.

Indeed, such uncritical support for nationalism blends with the desire of the Trotskyists to see capitalism restored in the Soviet Union. Outflanking even Workers Power, the Revolutionary Communist Party outlines explicitly the hidden agenda of the Trotskyist left:

> 'Whatever the short-term cost of capitalist restoration in the Stalinist world, the destruction of Stalinism will remove an historic barrier to the self-emancipation of the international working class.'
>
> FRANK RICHARDS, CONFRONTATION No 5

Fortunately for them, it is not the RCP who are having to pay the 'short-term cost' of capitalist restoration in, for example, the former GDR or Poland, in terms of mass unemployment, loss of housing and widespread poverty. 'Short-term', in these cases, means the ruination of many people's lives. However, far from the 'cost' being 'short-term', the restoration of capitalism in Eastern Europe has given a tremendous boost to imperialism.

The RCP's position – the restoration of capitalism in the Soviet Union would be a step forward for the international working class – does at least have the virtue of being honest – if stupid! *Socialist Outlook*, as befits these clandestine Labour Party entrists, are better at dissembling:

> 'Some will argue that to advocate independence is in effect to advocate independent capitalist states given the nature of the Popular Fronts. Such positions reveal both a profound pessimism and a lack of clarity on how socialists should support national movements.'
>
> DAFYDD RHYS, SOCIALIST OUTLOOK 1990

To read this article one would not imagine that a whole series of counter-revolutionary setbacks has put imperialism on the offensive, and the line is put that a 'clear space' exists for 'a common struggle against the Stalinist bureaucracy and imperialism.'

How the independence movements are going to take on the world or what the consequences might be are, wisely, left implicit. Presumably the nationalist movements are going to promote a political revolution which will finally overthrow that icon of Trotskyist demonology, the 'Stalinist bureaucracy'. The Soviet Union can then become a *real* threat to imperialism. That would be logical, if so utterly abstract as to bear little relation to reality. However, earlier on *Socialist Outlook* gives the actual reason for supporting the independence movements: if we do not we will be isolated:

> ' . . . Socialists have to not only support but advocate independence for these countries. Any other position would leave us by-passed by events and completely isolated from a dialogue with the masses.'

This is the same argument which the Trotskyists use to justify their continuous perambulations in and around the Labour Party and just as opportunist. Marxist politics should be characterised by political independence rather than tailing popular ideological formations, and their organisational expressions. In fact, given that a dialogue between *Socialist Outlook* and the nationalists is somewhat remote, one can surmise that their real concern is to tailor their position to accommodate their Labour Party audience.

One argument against a denial of the right to independence to the Soviet republics is that it is pandering to Great Russian chauvinism. Lenin is quite clear that one's position is relativist and is governed by the nature of the regime in question and the nation one is living in. The Polish debate again provides some useful guidelines. Lenin argues:

'The Polish Social Democrats cannot, at the moment, raise the slogan of Poland's independence, for the Poles, as proletarian internationalists, can do *nothing* about it without stooping . . . to humble servitude to *one* of the imperialist monarchies . . . The situation is, indeed, bewildering, but there is a way in which *all* participants would remain internationalists: the Russian and German Social Democrats by demanding for Poland unconditional *"freedom* to secede"; the Polish Social Democrats by working for the unity of the proletarian struggle in both small and big countries without putting forward the slogan of Polish independence for the given epoch or the given period.'

There are no exact parallels here from which to derive tactics. But it is clear that communists in the republics are correct to oppose independence, as otherwise they would be in 'humble servitude' to reactionary independence movements which are completely oriented towards imperialism. Communists in the imperialist countries can take note of the socialist credentials of the Soviet Union, which are under heavy internal attack but are still substantially extant, and conclude that there is a legitimacy in defending the integrity of a socialist state which would not exist in the case of an 'imperialist monarchy'. These tactical arguments do not transcend the strategic argument that the building of socialism takes precedence over the freedom to secede but they do reinforce it.

47

Lenin stresses the distinction between oppresed and oppressor nations. This distinction is not, at least in economic terms, a characteristic of the USSR. In fact, in an ideal world (such as the Trotskyists inhabit) it would be a useful exercise to grant the fractious republics immediate independence but *without* access to Soviet aid which has been extremely favourable to them. Neither is it likely that the imperialists would be prepared to pump large amounts of finance into such fragile allies. Poland has made many requests for aid but remarkably little has been actually forthcoming. Possibly the salutary lessons embodied here would lead to a voluntary reunion in the long run which would certainly be preferable to the present hostile situation. Unfortunately, such a scenario is quickly revealed as naive when the weakness of the Soviet Union relative to imperialism is considered.

To advocate an absolutist position of 'independence at any price', as most of the Trotskyists do, is also to advocate the final break up of the Soviet Union and the final destruction of the gains of 1917. No amount of mealy-mouthed talk should be allowed to suppress this fact. Such a result would be a mighty victory for imperialism, and all the more so as it would have been won at so little cost. In this situation the interests of the international working class and oppressed masses clearly take precedence over national aspirations in the Soviet republics. ▪

PART TWO

The crisis of socialism

2.1 EASTERN EUROPE 1989: SOCIALISM IN RETREAT
EDDIE ABRAHAMS
FRFI 92 · JANUARY 1990

The momentous changes, sweeping so rapidly across the socialist countries of Eastern Europe, are fundamentally altering the context in which the communist movement developed its strategy and tactics over the past four or five decades. With bewildering speed many old and seemingly unshakeable certainties are being challenged and hurled into irrelevance. Almost overnight the bourgeoisie sighs with tremendous relief. According to it, the main threat to bourgeois property and its attendant 'civilization' – communism – has proved to be only a transient spectre, a failure now vanishing into history.

Peaceful counter-revolution

To a greater or lesser extent, in Hungary, in Poland and Czechoslovakia, in the German Democratic Republic and in Bulgaria, a dangerous counter-revolutionary process has been unleashed. Many will find it hard to believe that counter-revolution can take the form of mass peaceful demonstrations on the streets calling for freedom. But it will become clear, as it already has in Poland, that those leading the movement are not intent on reforming and revitalising the socialist system but sweeping it away and with it all the gains the working class has made in those countries – social welfare, full employment, housing, education and health.

The commitment to freedom of the influential petit bourgeois sectors leading this movement will soon prove secondary to the priority of capital accumulation. In Poland Lech Walesa has argued that the Solidarity-led government should be given sweeping powers to push economic reforms through by decree in order to overcome delays in parliament.

This has happened now for two reasons. First, the reactionaries have seized the moment at which the Soviet Union has made clear its inability to sustain and defend socialism in Eastern Europe. Secondly, the leaders of these movements have been able to exploit the profound alienation of the Communist Parties from the working class with the latter playing a passive role in the political life of countries in Eastern Europe.

By exploiting the profound disenchantment with and hostility to the ruling Communist Parties, these counter-revolutionary elements were able to play a key role in mobilising the mass movement and in taking its leadership. In one form or another these movements (Solidarity in Poland, New Forum in the GDR, the Civic Forum in Czechoslovakia and the Union of Democratic Forces in Bulgaria) have effectively ended Communist Party rule.

Under the guise of advocating some generic non-class 'reform' to 'benefit all' the organised opposition in Eastern Europe is conducting a conscious pro-imperialist class battle on the economic and political front. They are demanding the replacement of the planned economy by a capitalist one, and the introduction of rights to allow them to organise independently of and in opposition to the working class.

Such 'reforms' stand in total contradiction to the interests of the majority of the population. Yet the success of the counter-revolutionaries in dragging hundreds of thousands behind this programme is testimony to the thorough degeneration of the ruling Communist Parties. They have lost all standing and respect among the people and have transformed once proud parties into vehicles for privilege and career. With the Communist Parties discredited and the working class lacking its own independent voice, the counter-revolutionaries are surging forward with unprecedented confidence.

The destruction of the planned economy

When urged to offer economic aid to the GDR, the West German Finance Minister, Theo Waigel refused: 'In no way will we finance the past or a new form of socialist planned economy in East Germany.' Chancellor Kohl pressed the point home by stating: 'Without a fundamental reform of the economic system, without scrapping the planned economy and erecting a market-based order, all assistance will be futile.'

The IMF, major imperialist banks and imperialist states are preparing proposals for multi-billion dollar aid packages to Eastern Europe. All these will be conditional on accelerating market reforms and privatisation, on austerity programmes and on price reforms which will eliminate subsidies on food and other essentials for the working class. The first results of such reforms can be seen in the unemployment queues and soup-kitchens in Poland. Here prices for bare essentials have rocketed and the population has been left hungry while meat is exported for foreign exchange to pay interest on staggering foreign debts.

The imperialist bourgeoisie recognise that socialism can finally be proclaimed dead only when the planned economies have been totally dismantled. They understand that politics is ultimately determined by economics and that the antithesis between capitalism and communism is to be found in the irreconcilable contradiction between the market and the planned economy. It is, therefore, to the destruction of the planned economy that they are directing their efforts, for as it collapses, so do all the obstacles standing in the way of predatory imperialist capital transforming the region into a pool of cheap labour and cheap raw materials. As a spokesperson for Fiat put it, Eastern Europe will be like the Third World, but on Europe's doorstep.

This imperialist economic programme is actively endorsed by the dominant and organised trend in the Eastern European opposition. The Czechoslovakian Civic Forum, for example, is: 'convinced that this (planned) economic system cannot be improved. We want to create a developed market . . . and real competition.' And an advisor adds that 'We need a Madame Thatcher here.'

In Bulgaria and East Germany the opposition has made market reforms a major plank of their platforms. In Hungary, the privatisation of the economy is being led by the ruling party itself. In Poland Lech Walesa, once the beloved of the British left, has offered Poland and its working class for sale to US and European capital. In the USA he appealed: 'We seek buyers for 80 per cent of the Polish economy . . . In Eastern Europe you can make the business deals of the century . . . '.

Alongside this reactionary economic programme, the counter-revolution has a clearly worked out political programme. In every Eastern European country we hear demands for an 'end to the leading role of the Communist Party', 'free elections', 'freedom of the press', 'freedom of conscience' etc. Running alongside these 'freedoms', are demands for prohibitions on any political organisation in the workplace. Anti-working class elements, whilst demanding freedom for themselves, try to stop the working class organising in its own interests.

The imposition of bourgeois 'freedoms' has already produced obscene and reactionary results. Proponents of capitalist restoration can now organise and act without fear of suppression. In the GDR, the fascist West German Republican Party is preparing to participate in 'democratic elections', and is distributing its leaflets on working class estates. Meanwhile pro-Nazi contingents are able to march on the weekly demonstrations in Leipzig. In Poland millionaires, and in their wake anti-Semitic fascists, unashamedly flaunt themselves in public life, while Jacek Kuron, Minister of Labour in the new Solidarity government, is preparing legislation to ban strikes.

The historical background to counter-revolution

To understand the origin and the survival of these counter-revolutionary forces it is necessary to turn to the legacy of 1945-1955: the period of the establishment of the socialist countries of Eastern Europe. The ruling Communist Parties proved too weak to eliminate the political, economic and social influence of the bourgeoisie and petit bourgeoisie. In agriculture, and even in industry, a significant proportion of the economy remained in bourgeois hands, while petit bourgeois social democratic elements infiltrated the state, the party and economic apparatus.

Socialism triumphed to a great extent because of the presence of the victorious Red Army, rather than as a result of working class uprisings. Unable to rule alone, Communist Parties, even the most powerful Czechoslovakian one, went through a process of mergers or federations with social democratic organisations which increased the weight of opportunism within the ruling parties. From the inception of socialism in Eastern Europe, therefore, the connection between the Communist Party and the working class was weak and already tainted by opportunist bureaucratic features. As a result of these factors, there was no thorough destruction of the old bourgeois state apparatus. The dictatorship of the proletariat was not exercised effectively and the working class was not drawn into active participation in running the planned economy and in political and social life. Bourgeois, bureaucratic and anti-democratic methods of government prevailed over the proletarian principles developed in the Paris Commune: the abolition of parliamentarianism and its replacement by direct working class democracy, the uniting of the legislative and executive arms of the state in the hands of an armed self-governing working class, the payment of only the average working class wage to state functionaries and working class delegates, the right of immediate recall of all party and state personnel.

Imperialism, therefore, had a strong foothold which it has used to undermine socialism. Through COCOM it prevented socialist countries gaining access to modern technology. Through its destructive arms-race it helped distort the socialist economies forcing them to divert key resources from civilian to military construction. With each major anti-imperialist and anti-capitalist victory, imperialism responded with savage war – Korea, Vietnam, Angola, Mozambique, Afghanistan, Kampuchea and elsewhere. In these conditions, it proved virtually impossible to develop the socialist economies internationally, let alone in Eastern Europe itself. These processes accelerated the already existing trend towards corruption, privilege and bureaucracy in the Communist Parties. Whilst accumulating the gross privileges recently exposed in the GDR and in Bulgaria, they stifled significant and honest working class criticism of these distortions. However, the anti-privilege current in the GDR, for example, is rapidly becoming an excuse for communist baiting. Nevertheless, today the Communist Parties do not have the political and moral strength to combat counter-revolution.

The future

Developments in Eastern Europe are by no means a foregone conclusion. Clearly, the anti-working class and anti-communist forces now have the initiative. But as the positive gains made by the Eastern European working class during the past four decades are undermined and as the capitalist market creates poverty and unemployment, once again the working class will begin to organise and resist.

Furthermore, during the next stage of its struggle, the working class, in Eastern Europe and internationally, starts from a higher level. Since the second imperialist war the working class has grown enormously not just in Eastern Europe, but in South Africa, in Latin America and South East Asia. So drunk is the bourgeoisie celebrating the retreat of socialism on one front, that it fails to see the millions upon millions who are digging its grave on the others. It does not see that the difficulties and problems presently confronting socialism are neither inherent nor inevitable but a product of imperialist warmongering, opportunist crimes and the mistakes the proletariat is bound to make on its road to final victory. It cannot see nor understand that as long as imperialism exists to exploit, oppress and murder, imperialism will never be left at peace and the masses will never cease to organise and fight for its destruction and for the ultimate liberation of humanity. In January 1919 on suppressing the German Revolution the ruling class expressed the same confidence as its kith and kin today. Rosa Luxemburg responded with a conviction based on her grasp of Marxism: ' "Order reigns in Berlin!" You stupid lackeys! Your "order" is built on sand. Tomorrow the revolution will rear its head once again, and, to your horror, will proclaim, with trumpets blazing: I was, I am, I will be!' ∎

2.2 EASTERN EUROPE: THE COLLAPSE OF SOCIALISM
EDDIE ABRAHAMS
FRFI 93 · FEBRUARY/MARCH 1990

The British ruling class, its servants in the Conservative and Labour parties and all its hacks in the media wildly applauded the collapse of the socialist system in Eastern Europe during the second half of 1989. The applause grew louder as they became more confident that, almost out of the blue, a massive market of over 400 million people was being opened up for plunder by capital.

The hard-nosed imperialist bourgeoisie, interested only in extracting profits and super-profits across the globe, has seen beyond all the nonsense about a 'glorious transition from totalitarianism to democracy'. 'This is the equivalent of the discovery by Europe of Latin America, exploiting cheap labour and cheap supplies' commented a senior Deutsche Bank economist. *The Financial Times* was equally frank arguing that, 'Low wage rates, at scarcely more than two dollars an hour even in relatively prosperous Czechoslovakia, are an attraction which could make these countries lucrative manufacturing centres.' The New York investment bankers, Morgan Stanley, confident of the pro-capitalist trend of development in Eastern Europe and the Soviet Union have announced that: 'It is time to invest heavily in this massive revolution.'

The first task of communists is to oppose this imperialist offensive. But, like the imperialists and opportunists, the British petit bourgeois left have welcomed developments failing to understand what is afoot is a fundamentally counter-revolutionary process setting the basis for a restoration of capitalism. The Socialist Workers Party (SWP), the Revolutionary Communist Party and the assortment of other Trotskyist groups within the Labour Party have deluded themselves, and are trying to delude others, into believing that

ROSA LUXEMBURG

'this is not a defeat for socialism but the defeat of Stalinism'. *Socialist Worker*, the newspaper of the SWP, sees the upheavals as 'the most powerful affirmation imaginable of the ability of ordinary working people to remake the world.'

Blinded by their petit bourgeois opposition to the socialist countries, British Trotskyists have applauded 'uprisings' against 'totalitarian' regimes, without caring to make a class analysis of the social and political forces involved. Blindly worshipping 'mass' movements, they refuse to examine the critical issue: which politically organised class forces stand at the head of the mass movement? These are petit-bourgeois and social democratic forces hostile to the working class and engaged in a conscious battle against socialism. They are consciously preparing to restore the market economy, cut subsidies on essential goods and services and invite in imperialist capital.

Communists do not ignore the deformations and distortions which existed in the socialist countries, yet we still recognise that recent developments represent a major setback for socialism. One only has to look at daily developments.

Within Eastern Europe, the reactionary, anti-working class character of the unfolding process is most evident in Poland and Hungary. On 1 January 1990, 20 separate bills became law in Poland setting the legal basis for the restoration of capitalism and the opening up of the country to imperialist capital. Overnight, working class living standards dropped by more than 30 per cent as subsidies on working class essentials were removed. Coal prices rose by 600 per cent, electricity by 500 per cent, bus and rail fares by 250 per cent, sugar by 300 per cent while bread prices are rising by 20 per cent a week. The Polish government has estimated that measures taken to rationalise and privatise the economy will create 400,000 unemployed workers in four months. But Jacek Kuron, Minister of Labour, admitted that this figure was 'pulled out of a hat' and that 'the IMF estimate is one million unemployed'. Employers have been given rights to sack workers en masse whilst the right to strike has been severely curtailed.

These austerity measures carried out at the behest of the IMF are no different from those the IMF forces upon the nations of the Third

World. They are designed to 'discipline' the working class and ensure both profits for imperialist investors and the repayment of Poland's £36 billion debt. The advantages once enjoyed by the Polish working class are fast vanishing. A Polish housewife states: 'We can't buy any clothes, we can't paint the kitchen; theatres, cinemas and holidays are out of the question now.' While a pensioner states: 'By the time we have paid our rent, electricity and heating we will have just enough for a couple of pounds of butter.'

In Hungary a similar process is under way, with an austerity plan freezing wages but raising rents by 50 per cent, food prices by 45 per cent, water by 300 per cent, and other public services, electricity and transport by 45 per cent. These measures accompany massive privatisations and unemployment.

Given such propitious conditions for capital accumulation, major imperialist powers, their companies and banks are preparing multi-billion pound credit deals and industrial investment projects. US, EC and Japanese imperialism are threatening to transform the region into a battleground as they fight for the best position from which to extract the greatest profit for themselves. When the Japanese Prime Minister visited Europe in January he provided $150 million to help Poland stabilise its currency and another $25 million for emergency food purchases. He also offered $500 million to each country in the form of export credits and a further $25 million for technical co-operation. Meanwhile the EC, and Germany in particular, are planning their own credit schemes hoping to outflank the Japanese.

Hundreds of imperialist firms are opening up offices in Poland and Hungary. In Hungary General Motors has taken a 67 per cent control-ling interest in the RABA truck firm, while General Electric has bought Tungstram, famous for its electrical equipment. In Poland Chase Enterprises is investing $900 million of cable systems whilst Fiat, Honda, Suzuki and Murdoch's and Maxwell's newspaper empires are all reparing lucrative deals.

What is happening in Poland and Hungary is a foretaste of what imperialism and its allies are planning for the whole of Eastern Europe.

On an international scale developments in Eastern Europe and the

Soviet Union have shifted the balance of forces in favour of imperialism and against socialism and national liberation movements. Speaking at the Council for Mutual Economic Assistance (CMEA – the socialist equivalent of the European Community) on 9 January 1990, Cuban Vice President Carlos Rafael Rodriguez noted that: 'The weakening of socialism as a system gives the imperialists added euphoria and arrogance'.

This euphoria stems from the fact that liberation movements and socialist countries in the Third World are experiencing serious isolation and weakness as once accessible sources of political, military and financial aid are closed off. Imperialism will thus become more confident and more aggressive in its striving for domination and profit.

Liberation movements such as the African National Congress, which once enjoyed support from Eastern European, now find these countries opening their doors to the racist apartheid regime. In January 1990 Pik Botha was welcomed in Hungary where he began negotiations to increase trade and economic collaboration. Simultaneously the apartheid regime has been allowed to wage a campaign to attract white labour from Eastern Europe to apartheid South Africa. The Palestinian people, and the PLO in particular, are also being abandoned in favour of the racist Zionist state. Poland and Hungary have resumed diplomatic relations with Israel which is sending its emissaries to mount a massive campaign to develop economic links and create a market for its commodities in the region.

Anti-imperialist and national liberation movements across the world which once enjoyed support from the socialist countries will now have to fight in much more difficult circumstances. Imperialism will be doubly ruthless. Fearing no significant response from the Soviet Union or Eastern Europe, it will use its awesome firepower to try and crush anti-imperialist movements.

In the immediate period ahead the socialist countries of the Third World stand to suffer most from the collapse of the socialist system. The basis for their independent economic development, already devastated by imperialist embargoes, low intensity warfare and sabotage, are now threatened further by the imminent collapse of the CMEA. The Cuban Vice President explained: 'One of the major accomplishments of the

CMEA is having introduced to the benefit of non-European members, preferential prices leading to the elimination of unequal terms of trade . . . '

These progressive relations are now threatened as Czechoslovakia prepares to leave CMEA and other nations including the Soviet Union demand a major restructuring of the organisation. The Soviet Union's Prime Minister Ryzhkov proposed the replacement of socialist economic relations with the demand that trade within CMEA be conducted in hard currency and at world market prices. If eventually implemented, such measures will have a devastating effect on the economies of countries like Cuba and Vietnam already suffering arbitrary price rises and interruption of urgent supplies from Eastern Europe.

Besides the imperialist ruling class, the only other force to benefit from developments in Eastern Europe has been social democracy: a pernicious, pro-imperialist, racist trend within the working class which we are familiar with in the form of the Labour Party. Within the working class in Eastern Europe, social democracy is replacing communism and socialism as the dominant trend. Rather than applauding such developments, communists should be consistently exposing the grave dangers they present to the working class internationally.

Social democracy's programme of a mixed-economy and a welfare state – ie, a benevolent capitalism – can be realised only for a tiny minority of the world's population. It can only be realised at the expense of the vast majority. It depends on the most savage imperialist exploitation and oppression of the Third World. This is the message communists must drive home. Only in this way can we target the international working class's real enemy – imperialism and British imperialism in particular. ■

2.3 POLAND: SOLIDARITY AND COUNTER-REVOLUTION
DAVID REED & MAXINE WILLIAMS
FRFI 15 · JANUARY 1982

'Our country is on the edge of the abyss. Achievements of many generations, raised from the ashes, are collapsing into ruin. State structures no longer function. New blows are struck each day at our weakened economy. Living conditions are oppressing people with growing burdens.'

With these words General Jaruzelski announced the introduction of martial law in Poland. This extreme measure had become necessary to defend the very existence of the socialist state. The RCG unreservedly defends the right of the socialist forces in Poland to take these measures.

For a whole period of time the imperialists have been actively fomenting pro-capitalist, anti-Soviet forces in Poland. Whilst hypocritically demanding that the Soviet Union 'keep out of Poland' the imperialists have for years past interfered in the political and economic affairs of Poland. They have used Poland's crippling indebtedness to the imperialist banks as a means of exerting greater and greater control over Poland's internal economic affairs. Today the expansion of industry, the building of houses, the standard of living of the Polish masses are held to ransom by the massive interest payments – $200 million per month – that Poland has to pay to the parasitic, bloodsucking imperialist banks.

Not content with bankrupting the Polish economy, the imperialists have actively aided the anti-Soviet opposition in Poland. The imperialists have found a willing tool for their schemes in the pro-imperialist trade union movements in Europe and the USA. The latter have channelled large amounts of equipment and other aid to Solidarity, the Polish trade union that has rapidly become the major instrument of counter-revolution in Poland. Organisations like the virulently right wing and racist US trade union, the AFL-CIO, set up a fund of $200,000 for Solidarity. Other countries' unions have followed suit including the reactionary British TUC. These unions joined with the neo-fascist Franz-Josef Strauss who donated DM1 million (nearly $200,000) to

Solidarity through his front organisation, the Hans Seidel Foundation. So much for 'non-intervention' by the imperialists. When Reagan, the imperialist butcher of the Salvadorean people, and Carrington, the smooth-tongued, imperialist defender of British torture in Ireland, champion trade union rights in Poland, honest people will look closely at what they are defending.

What is Solidarity?

It is a strange trade union which argues for a programme which would lead to unemployment. Yet Solidarity, with massive Western support, has put its weight behind measures which, if implemented, would lead to an end to full employment in Poland. A brief look at the main planks of its programme shows that Solidarity has taken a pro-capitalist direction:

An end to central planning
'Socialised concerns should be given the freedom to determine their production plans and methods ... the centralised distribution of raw materials and other elements of production should be limited and even-tually done away with ... the concerns should be self-financing ... they should be evaluated not on the basis of fulfilling the plan, but on the basis of economic efficiency ... The self management bodies ... should should have the right to exercise control over the assets of the con-cern, to decide on the aims of production and sales, the choice of production methods, and investment goals. They should also decide on the distribution of the profits of the enterprise.'

Capitalist competition
' ... a precondition of the proper functioning of an enterprise under the new system is the de-mono-

SOLIDARITY SUPPORTERS

polisation of the market and the appearance of competing producers to a certain extent.'

Capitalist (Kulak) agriculture

'... it is particularly necessary to eliminate all restrictions on the development of family farms and family owned handicraft and service shops ... Full respect for the private ownership of land by individual farmers ...'

The freedom to be unemployed

'The union recognises that the enterprises will have the right to make changes in their employment level as they need to. But the government authorities will still be responsible for carrying out a full employment policy, although this policy must no longer hinder productive concerns ... the self-financing of the enterprise may also result in some having to cut back or close down ...'

This is a petit bourgeois programme for the restoration of a kind of 'welfare capitalism'. Central planning is to go. Workers in every firm will compete with workers in other firms. Capitalist enterprise should be allowed to compete with socialism. Private farming is to be encouraged. Firms can hire or fire workers according to free market criteria. Lenin said of such proposals in his own time:

'Any direct or indirect legalisation of the rights of ownership of the workers of any given factory or any given trade on their particular production, or of their right to weaken or impede the orders of the state authority, is a flagrant distortion of the basic principles of Soviet power and a complete rejection of socialism.'

CW, VOL 42, p100

The Solidarity programme represents just such a complete rejection of socialism. One week before martial law was declared Lech Walesa himself admitted at a meeting at Radom where leaders of Solidarity were discussing plans to overthrow the state:

'They are well aware that if we implement our programme, that if we distribute the land from state farms to private peasants and create self-management committees everywhere, we will be dismantling their system.

That they intended to take steps to overthrow the socialist state is clear. Warsaw Solidarity leader Zbigniew Bujak was quoted as saying that the first action of the workers militia had to be 'aimed at liberating' the radio and television centre, establishment of a 'social council for the national economy' which would be 'something like a provisional national government', overthrowing the present government.

Indeed when Solidarity was set up the leading influences were a well known group of anti-socialist dissident intellectuals like Jacek Kuron, who wished to use the power of the Polish working class as a battering ram to destroy the Polish state and implement their own programme for the restoration of capitalism.

The Polish Communist Party (PUWP) and Solidarity

Honest communists faced with these developments must ask how they came about. How was it possible for KOR and right-wing Solidarity leaders to use the legitimate grievances of the Polish workers for their own counter-revolutionary ends? This is a question for the Polish Communists to resolve through dialogue with the Polish people when the immediate threat to the Polish state is at an end. General Jaruzelski has already accepted that the failures, mistakes, and in some cases the personal corruption of leading Communist Party members over the past decade have contributed to the crisis and to the Communist Party's disastrous divorce from the trade union movement encompassing millions of working people. It is this divorce which has allowed bourgeois and petit bourgeois influences like KOR to masquerade as the friends of the Polish workers. The Communist Party failed to overcome this divorce by politically winning the workers so that they, together with the Communist Party, could confront the problems faced by the country. Instead, it took to borrowing massively from the imperialist banks in a vain attempt to buy itself out of the crisis.

In 1981, Fidel Castro clearly pointed to the danger of this:

'Especially in Poland, imperialism is orchestrating a sinister act of provocation directed against the socialist camp. The success that reaction has had there is eloquent testimony to the fact that the revolutionary party in power cannot deviate from Marxist-Leninist principles, neglect ideological work and divorce itself from the masses; and, when the time for rectification comes, this should not be done on the basis of concessions to the class enemy, either inside or outside the country.'

Which side are you on?

The events in Poland raise one central question – which side are you on? On the one side are the socialist states defending the gains of the working class and aiding the movements fighting imperialism throughout the world. On the other side is imperialism, intent on destroying socialism, crushing the working class and defeating liberation movements. Without significant exception the British middle class socialists have joined the Labour Party and trade union movement in taking the side of imperialism. The CPGB and the Trotskyist left (SWP, IMG, WRP et al) have lined up in outright support for the counter-revolution in Poland and have condemned the Soviet Union and its Polish allies.

Whilst real communists put revolutionary interest higher than formal democracy, the CPGB calls for the release of counter-revolutionaries in Poland under the guise of supporting democratic rights. This same Communist Party has *never* called for the release of Irish political prisoners from British prisons. *Socialist Worker* calls on Polish workers to 'go into the streets to confront the military forces' in order to seize political power and overthrow the Polish socialist state. This from an organisation that refused to mobilise its own membership in defence of the Irish hunger strikers and which has consistently condemned the revolutionary war of the IRA against British imperialism.

These organisations always defend British imperialism and reserve their most virulent attacks for the determined forces of socialism and liberation. It will be of interest to *Fight Racism! Fight Imperialism!* readers to know that these organisations which have refused to bring out their members on demonstrations in support of the Irish revolution, have within days taken steps to mobilise for an anti-Soviet demonstration on the events in Poland. At this demonstration, they will line up with a platform of Tories and Labour imperialists including Sir Bernard Braine, Peter Shore (right-wing Labour), Shirley Williams and Eric Heffer (well known for his refusal to support Irish hunger strikers in their struggle for freedom.)

Imperialists hands off socialist Poland!

Communists in Britain reject the anti-socialist campaign of the imperialists and their Labour and left allies. British banks led by Barclays and Lloyds have claims of £1 billion on the Polish people. The RCG calls for the liquidation of all Polish debts to British banks. A movement in this country, capable of enforcing this, would make a real contribution to the freedom of the Polish people.

If Solidarity were to succeed, then Poland would be turned into a base for the counter-revolution against the whole socialist camp. Any imperialist inroads into the socialist countries would set back the struggle of the vast majority of mankind for a life free from poverty, oppression and racism. It is the Soviet Union and its allies that give financial and military support to the liberation movements fighting imperialism in Southern Africa, Central America, the Middle East and elsewhere. The RCG defends the right of the Soviet Union and the Polish Communist Party to take whatever steps are necessary to ensure that Poland remains in the socialist camp. ■

2.4 POLAND: SOLIDARITY TAKES POWER
EDDIE ABRAHAMS
FRFI 89 · SEPTEMBER 1989

The Polish Communist Party (formally known as the PUWP – Polish United Workers Party) has peacefully surrendered power to the bourgeois and counter-revolutionary forces at the head of Solidarity. On Thursday 24 August 1989, the Sejm (Polish Parliament), with only four Communists voting against, confirmed Solidarity lawyer and journalist Tadeuz Mazowiecki as Prime Minister. Anti-communist and anti-socialist Solidarity leader Lech Walesa expressed precisely the political significance of this development: 'Nobody has previously taken the road that leads from socialism to capitalism. We are setting out to do just that.'

The imperialists and their allies in Poland were jubilant. Newspaper headlines informed us of the 'end of communism', the 'collapse of the Soviet empire' and the beginning of 'democracy and freedom'. Bronislaw Geremek, representing Solidarity's almost fascist trend, said:

'For the first time in 45 years, a Polish government is to be formed on Polish soil, by non-communist forces. The monopoly of the Party which ruled Poland against the will of the people has been broken.'

The Polish people however were not cheering. Even bourgeois observers noted that there was 'little evidence of jubilation', the people having 'run out of enthusiasm' for Solidarity and for politics in general. They are concerned more with the massive prices rises on essential items that flow from the 'market reforms' which the new government is bent on accelerating.

Mazowiecki, at his inauguration, proclaimed that we would strive for 'really innovative solutions' to Poland's vast economic problems and foreign debt of $40 billion. These amounted to nothing more than 'implementing the market economy' and systematically dismantling the once socialist foundations of Poland's economy. The new government will moved to abolish all subsidies and lift all price controls. It will accelerate the process of selling off socially-owned forces of production to the parvenu Polish bourgeoisie or to international capital. In addition, loss-making firms will be closed down and unemployment will increase dramatically. While a tiny minority will thus continue to enrich itself, the majority of the working class will again begin to experience biting poverty and hunger. Is it at all surprising that this 'freedom and democracy' to make a minority rich is greeted with indifference by the majority?

The imperialists meanwhile are turning a deaf ear to the new government's request for $10 billion aid for the next three years. Rather than bailing out the Polish economy with aid, Bush and Thatcher want it opened up even further and more resolutely to private imperialist capital. They are confident that their lackeys in Solidarity will toe the line. That the workers and the poor will suffer bothers them not at all. All they are interested in is repayments on Poland's debt and investment opportunities for their capitalists and financiers.

The future of socialism

It is a tragedy for Polish and international communism that the Polish Communist Party proved incapable of winning the confidence and loyalty of the Polish working class. Disillusioned with the PUWP it turned to Solidarity whose bourgeois leadership manipulated and exploited, for its own counter-revolutionary ends, the genuine grievances of the Polish working class.

As the Party lost its working class support, it was more or less captured by elements in the state and industrial apparatus who, to preserve their own privileges and enrich themselves, turned to the capitalist road. In a significant article, Daniel Passent, deputy editor of *Polityka*, the Communist Party newspaper, wrote:

'Ever since Solidarity's birth in 1980 the Party has been in retreat. The *Communist Manifesto* has been shelved and nobody mentions the dictatorship of the proletariat [while] Party newspapers and politicians praise the private and market economy instead of the state one . . . '

As a result, the Party became 'an organisation of directors, managers and officers' totally divorced from the working class. It was used, by its leading personnel, as a vehicle to secure a position for themselves in a bourgeois Poland. Stories of Communist Party members who were managers and directors of state enterprises taking them over as private property are legion. It is not surprising that such a Party is hated and treated with contempt.

Despite these terrible developments, socialism in Poland is by no means dead. Let us quote again from Daniel Passent's article:

'The left in Poland will not perish completely. Socialism left durable traces in people's consciousness. The trend towards reprivatisation – the re-establishment of private schools, the rich villas and limousines of the new bourgeoisie, the Church's great influence, the revival of right-wing nationalism and obscurantism, deeper and deeper poverty and the spectre of unemployment in a market economy – will create a climate for the left's revival. This will be a new left, smaller but more authentic than the traditional model of the past . . . '

Developments in Poland are being watched closely by capitalist and working class forces internationally. In the socialist countries in particular, the working class movement will study with care the fate of its comrades in Poland. And as it sees the depredations and devastations wrought by the market reforms, it will hopefully reject those who are proposing the same for their own countries.   ■

2.5 EAST GERMANY: THE FIRST ANNIVERSARY OF COLONISATION
CLAUDIA (BERLIN)
FRFI 104 · DECEMBER/JANUARY 1991/92

---

3 October 1991: East Germany (or 'the five new *länder*', as it is affectionately called by its Western patrons) is supposed to celebrate the first anniversary of its initiation into freedom, wealth and democracy. Strangely enough, there is no trace of celebration anywhere, no fire-

works – just the odd demonstration in Berlin against xenophobia and racist violence.

So how come there is so little enthusiasm for the united Germany? West Germans, on the one hand, are annoyed that unity is costing money. They have to pay a new sort of tax called *Solidaritätsabgabe* to sponsor unity! East Germans, on the other hand, have to understand that they will remain the 'Ossies'; the underdogs of the country, for a long time to come.

Rather than bringing people together, this first year of unity has shown them how different they are – and the differences are growing. Surveys show that more than 50 per cent of East Germans feel colonised by West Germany. So let's take a close look at this new colony Germany North-East. Does this colonisation follow the old rules?

Expropriation of the natives

There are 1.3 million applicants for the restitution of land and buildings. In East Berlin, every tenth estate is claimed by former owners (often war criminals who were expropriated after the war and moved west); in many other communities it is one in three. In extreme cases, up to ten owners-to-be are competing for the same attractive plot. Nobody cares for the residents of the past 40 years.

The restitution of the former national property of the GDR follows the same pattern. Three quarters of what was privatised by the *Treuhandanstalt* was handed over to West Germans. No single enterprise employing more than 1,000 people went to an East German.

The same picture in agriculture. East Germans don't have the money to buy the land they've been cultivating for decades.

Raiding the country

Normally territory is colonised in order to strip it of its minerals and other goodies. In East Germany, there are no precious stones or other valuable raw materials, but there is something quite useful within the EC: production quotas allotted to factories. By buying up sugar factories in the East, for example, West German competitors get the quota as well. Then when Eastern factories are closed down, the production quotas are transferred to the West.

'Jungle Bonus' for the expeditionary forces

West German civil servants who go to the East to set up new structures are entitled to a bonus of 1,500 to 2,500DM a month – a taxfree bonus that is higher than the monthly income of many East Germans.

Taking over the administration

As East Germans supposedly did not know how to run a country, scores of advisers and administrators were sent East to turn local administration, and the legal and education systems upside down to then elevate it to Western levels . . .

Protecting domestic economy from competitors

What do you do with East German factories that are capable of competing with their Western counterparts? You close them down – as happened to the NARVA light bulb manufacturer which would have made a mess of the market Osram and Philips had so neatly divided between themselves.

Exporting waste to the colony

France became notorious for exporting toxic waste to its former colonies in West Africa. For a couple of dollars, highly toxic chemicals were dumped in villagers' backyards. In the same way, East Germany is seen as a backyard for West German waste. Greenpeace found out that 150,000 tons of toxic waste from the West were illegally dumped in 1990 on one site alone. On other dumps the waste was just marked as 'household refuse'.

Glass beads for the natives

It started with bananas in November 1989. After monetary union, it continued with second-hand cars, and now it is dubious insurance and investment funds that inexperienced Easterners are talked into. So far, East Germans have lost 1 billion Marks to smart 'investment advisers'.

Destroying the culture

By the end of the year, there will be no more GDR television and radio. The first GDR TV station was taken over as early as a year ago; the remainder will follow suit. Many libraries, cultural centres and youth clubs were closed down – the communities cannot finance them any more. Gone are the days of generous state subsidies for culture, artists and the arts . . . Video rentals are coming to the culture-starved natives' aid and are offering the full range of sex and crime, all these highlights of Western culture people in the East had been deprived of . . . Writer Christa Wolf points to the fatal consequences of the colonisation of GDR culture in order to 'demonise the real history of those who lived in the GDR and let it disappear in a dark hole of oblivion.' ∎

2.6 THE CRISIS OF SOCIALISM IN CHINA
TREVOR RAYNE
FRFI 88 · JULY/AUGUST 1989

'Between cities, messages fly through fax machines in friendly offices, and the latest stories in US and European newspapers arrive within hours. Shortwave broadcasts of the Voice of America . . . beam news reports in Chinese. Hotel satellite dishes draw down . . . virtually all the major US network news shows. When one US professor went to take a look at demonstrators, a student greeted him with this question "How much play is ABC News giving us?" ' THE WALL STREET JOURNAL, 30 MAY 1989

As communists we strongly criticise the indiscriminate shooting of students that took place in Beijing on 3-4 June. The People's Liberation Army (PLA) operation was an expression of the crisis of communism in China, and of the failure of the Communist Party of China (CPC) to give leadership in the struggle for socialism. It threatens to undermine the Chinese people's support for the socialist system.

The path of reform introduced by Deng Xiaoping has reduced state ownership of the means of production and distribution, diminished the role of planning in the economy and removed the state monopoly of

71

foreign trade. Chinese foreign policy has often been opportunistically nationalistic: supporting counter-revolutionaries in Afghanistan and Kampuchea, attacking socialist Vietnam and favouring US imperialism against the Soviet Union. The result of these violations of socialist principles has been the exacerbation of class differences in Chinese society, the elevation of the market and profit motive in directing resources and the diminution of socialist class consciousness and education. In particular, urban Chinese youth have been encouraged by the Chinese government's policies to value capitalist commodity culture above service to the liberation of the working class and humanity.

Unlike much of the British left, *Fight Racism! Fight Imperialism!* does not glorify the student movement. The students' demands for democracy, a free press, human rights and an end to corruption were abstract and given no specific working class content. There was no evidence of students criticising Deng's reformist programme from a revolutionary perspective, and no evidence, beyond the singing of the *Internationale*, of their solidarity with the struggles of the world's oppressed in Palestine, South Africa, El Salvador etc. Rather, they identified with Solidarity in Poland. It is clear that counter-revolutionaries took leading positions in the student movement, and are now in refuge with imperialism in Hong Kong and the USA. Several student organisations had links with pro-Kuomintang groups based in Taiwan, Hong Kong and the USA, and received funds from them. A record 40,000 Chinese students are studying in the USA: half from the People's Republic, half from Taiwan. Contacts have been manipulated by imperialism. Fang Lizhi, a leading ideologue of the student movement, openly anti-Marxist, said to a gathering earlier this year that he hoped 'that entrepreneurs, as China's new rising force, will join with the advanced intellectuals to fight for democracy'. Calls for a multi-party system and the downfall of the CPC emerged in the student movement. Until two years ago, Fang, now sheltering in the US embassy in Beijing, was a CPC member.

Nevertheless, a million people filed through Tiananmen Square in mid-May: workers, soldiers and party officials among them. Deng's reforms inevitably generated two tendencies in the student movement: one anti-socialist, demanding the political changes that would allow an acceleration of capitalist restoration; the other, representative of the victims of this process, the working class and poorer peasants, opposed to the growing manifestations of capitalism – inflation, corruption, inequalities, etc. These two trends surfaced within the leadership of the CPC, together with a group even to the right of Deng around former General Secretary Zhao Ziyang. Their dispute paralysed the Party and worsened the confusion among students and workers alike. With no clear political line, the student movement was in danger of falling into the hands of counter-revolution. The imperialist media intervened with rumour and distortion. When the PLA acted it was met with fierce resistance; many soldiers were brutally killed. That it had to act at all is testimony to the paralysis and confusion in the CPC. Some 300-700 civilians were killed, not the several thousands that the imperialist media originally claimed.

On 13 June premier Li Peng announced that China's economic and foreign policies would not change. The PLA's demonstration of military power will not be enough to seize-up socialism. There is a very great danger that counter-revolution will flourish both within and without the CPC if past policies are continued.

China's 'Open Door'.

When the Polish government blood-lessly instituted martial law in 1981, imperialism responded vehemently with wide-ranging sanctions. When it comes to China in 1989 Bush and Thatcher, promoters of death squads in Central America and Ireland, mouth a few hypocritical criticisms and proceed with business as usual. Capital is making a large investment in China; Deng Xiaoping opened the

CHINA, 1989

73

door for it in 1978 with the Four Modernisations programme.

Eighty per cent of China's 1.1 billion people are peasants. Socialism requires a high level of development of the productive forces and a productivity, beyond that achieved by capitalism. For as long as capital has a higher productivity its cheap commodities represent a threat to the development of socialist production. They provide a potential material base for a counter-revolutionary alliance between wealthier peasants, the petit bourgeois and bourgeois elements in society with imperialism. Against this must be state control of trade, and an alliance of the working class and poor and middle peasants under the leadership of the Communist Party.

When the Soviet Union launched its planned economy in 1928, its steel output was 3.3 times that of China in 1952 and its oil output 29 times greater. China had four times as many people, but produced only twice as much grain. Building socialism under such conditions was a tremendous problem, compounded by the sheer weight of peasant agriculture in the economy and the Chinese break with the Soviet Union in the early 1960s. Chairman Mao Zedong's solution, promoted during the Great Leap Forward 1957-59, and the Cultural Revolution 1966-76, was to collectivise agriculture, reduce income differentials in industry and place 'politics in command' encouraging the poor peasants, working class and students to struggle against bourgeois privilege. Collectivised farming would free labour for industrialisation and construction, and industry would develop at a pace determined by the modernisation of farming. Opposing Mao were those he dubbed 'the number one and two capitalist roaders'; Lin Shaoqi and Deng Xiaoping. For Lin and Deng collectivisation was unthinkable before agriculture was mechanised. A free market in land would accelerate development. At the same time emphasis should be placed on building heavy industry and the use of material incentives. Both lines face the same problem: how can enough surplus be accumulated to allow industrial investment without forcing down the level of peasant consumption, and thereby threatening the peasant-worker alliance that maintains the socialist state?

Deng's Four Modernisations (science and technology, agriculture, industry and national defence) are designed to make China a leading industrial nation by the year 2000. They have involved the decollectivisation of agriculture, encouragement of private plots, the introduction of capitalist management techniques and hierarchies in industry, productivity bonus schemes, profit and loss accounting as measures of efficiency, the displacement of 'surplus labour', and the introduction of modern technology through monopoly capital investment. The importation of foreign capital was always an option for speeding up industrialisation. China's economy has grown at 11 per cent per annum since 1982. Its share of world trade has doubled to 1.6 per cent over ten years. However, 70 per cent of that trade is with imperialism; in the 1950s a similar proportion took place with the socialist countries. At the same time, US companies have invested $4 billion in China; capital has poured in from Japan, West Germany and Hong Kong: Tootal, Pilkington, BSR, Cable and Wireless and a string of other British firms have investments. Today, state-owned industries account for less than 64 per cent of industrial output compared with 83 per cent in 1978. Taxes recouped from state-owned concerns are now down 38 per cent on 1988 revenues. Investment in agriculture fell from 11.1 per cent of total spending in 1979 to 3.4 per cent in 1985.

State control of the economy is weakening. Inevitably, capitalism has spontaneously reasserted itself, creating unemployment, inflation (now at 30 per cent), impoverishment and cuts in welfare expenditure, alongside grotesque inequalities and luxury consumption.

Capitalist mayhem

'People regard a job as a taxi driver as better than that of a doctor, not because egalitarian principles operate in China, but because a taxi driver earns more than a doctor or a university lecturer.'
NEW SCIENTIST, 3 JUNE 1989

As central government deficits increase, provincial government revenues have grown. Regional disparities are increasing particularly between the wealthier coastal regions and poorer mountainous interior.

Four special economic zones for capitalist investment have been established. In Guangdong, which neighbours Hong Kong, up to three million workers are supplied by government agencies to 60,000 Hong Kong-based companies. A young woman employed by these firms earns twice the pay of a worker in a state enterprise, but half that paid by the same firm to its employees in Hong Kong. Capital appears as a source of prosperity. Hong Kong dollars are widely used throughout Guangdong; laws modelled on those used in Japan and the USA have been introduced to regulate labour and job security has been removed for many workers. Bankruptcy and taxation laws have been imported from Hong Kong, as have the customary practices of bribery, under-invoicing and buying and selling of shares as a means of extracting a portion of value without working oneself.

While luxury consumption has increased, education has been starved of funds. Almost 35 per cent of people over 15 are illiterate or semi-literate. Teachers go unpaid while hotels and golf-courses are built. A state employed architect, doctor or engineer is likely to earn around £20 a month. A market stall holder selling produce from a private plot earns 15 or 25 times as much as a teacher. The young woman employed by an electronics transnational in Guangdong will get about twice as much as the state doctor. University places go vacant, people do not train as doctors. Children are leaving school below the minimum age of 15 to work their family plots. Richer peasants buy up additional land, hire the labour of poorer or dispossessed peasants and spend their fortunes on imported capitalist luxuries. This alliance between a section of the population and imperialism is real and it extends into the CPC itself! Little wonder that Communist Party officials have referred to themselves as running a 'South Korean economic model'. Zhao Ziyang, now dismissed CPC General Secretary favoured by the students, was a chief proponent of the Guangdong project.

What were intended as joint Chinese state/foreign capital ventures are becoming solely imperialist capital operations; joint enterprises scheduled for several years are turning into several decades; Chinese labour increasingly produces for the capitalist market while trans-nationals freely exploit Chinese consumption; profits made by transnationals are entirely remitted to the imperialist heartlands.

'Black cat, white cat, who cares, as long as it catches the mice', Deng Xiaoping once said when asked about encouraging private enterprise as a means of development. The student protest must indicate to the CPC the dangers of trying to build socialism with capitalist methods: it cannot be done. The increasingly capitalist content of Chinese society now threatens to destroy its socialist form. China's working class is now 130 million strong. Revolutionary communists within the CPC must seek to win back the confidence of the working class and mobilise its democratic demands for power, education, health care and higher living standards against the beneficiaries of Deng's policies. Above all, they must fight to re-establish the barrier against imperialism that the socialist state served as. It was won in 1949 after 20 million Chinese workers and peasants had died fighting the imperialist armies and their Kuomintang stooges. Imperialism will gladly shed another 20 million Chinese lives if it can achieve counter-revolution.   ■

2.7 AFGHANISTAN: COUNTER-REVOLUTION VICTORIOUS
BOB SHEPHERD
FRFI 107 · JUNE/JULY 1992

---

25 April 1992 saw the culmination of 14 years of imperialist-backed counter-revolution in Afghanistan as the forces of the Islamic Jihad Council took power in Kabul. The ruling Homeland Party, formerly known as the People's Democratic Party of Afghanistan (PDPA), racked by divisions had ousted President Najibullah from its leadership on 16 April. It had lost effective control of strategic areas of the country as sections of the armed forces had defected to the Mojahedin. The collapse of socialism in the old Soviet Union had meant an end to military aid to Afghanistan and a weakening of the power of the armed forces. This had led Najibullah to agree to a UN peace plan for Afghanistan, which proposed that power pass to a council of 15 'neutral' Afghans at the end of April, followed by the formation of a transitional government. The defection of sections of the armed forces

to the counter-revolutionary Mojahedin undermined the position of Najibullah and sealed the fate of the Afghan government.

Since the Revolution of April 1978, imperialism had set its sights on the destruction of the progressive government in Kabul. They were intent on restoring to power the feudal landlords and capitalists who had held the Afghan people in bondage. Reagan and Thatcher financed and encouraged the development of the Mojahedin. In 1978, before the Soviet intervention of 1979, the CIA had established 30 bases for training Afghan terrorists. They received more financial backing from the USA than the Contras in Nicaragua, over $2 billion from the CIA in ten years. The targets of the Mojahedin were schools, hospitals, agricultural and industrial projects. Between 1981 and 1985 they destroyed nearly 2,000 schools, 30 hospitals and 100 health clinics. The war has devastated the country with over one million dead and five million refugees in Pakistan and Iran.

After the Soviet intervention to defend the gains of the Revolution in 1979, imperialism used the dirty war of the Mojahedin not just to undermine the Afghan Revolution, but as a weapon against the Soviet Union itself. As the US ambassador to Pakistan between 1988 and 1991 put it: 'Afghanistan is the place where the Reagan doctrine paid off . . . The unravelling of the cold war began there.'

Before the 1978 revolution, Afghanistan was a desperately poor, backward country. 85 per cent of the population lived on the land and felt the brunt of poverty. 40 per cent of all arable land was owned by four per cent of the population. Over 50 per cent of peasant families were in massive debt to landlords and moneylenders because their land-holdings were too small to make ends meet. The per capita income of Afghans was just $157 a year in 1978.

Only 0.65 per cent of the GNP was spent on health care: with only one doctor per 15,000 people, life expectancy was 42 years for men and 43 for women. Afghanistan ranked 119th in the world in terms of health care, and 127th in the world in terms of education. The illiteracy rate before the Revolution was 98 per cent: in the ten years before the Revolution 5,265 people had learnt to read and write! Immediately following the Revolution, the government of the PDPA issued laws which enshrined equality between men and women and banned forced marriages. For the first time women were elected onto local bodies of power. The government instigated land reform, putting a limit on an individual's right to private ownership of land, and cancelled peasant debts. All nationalities were granted equal rights and prestige, with education taking place in the language of national minorities.

All these measures were detested by the reactionary Mojahedin and were the targets of their attacks. Now they have taken power, all the progressive laws introduced by the PDPA will be reversed. A reactionary, anti-communist regime in Kabul is already attacking women's rights and has begun the slaughter of communists. Karim Shardan, former chief minister of justice, was kidnapped, tortured and murdered in Kabul on 3 May. Abdul Ghorbandi, a leading member of the Homeland Party, was also kidnapped, but rescued the same day. On 8 May, leader of the Jamiat-i-Islami Party Rabbani announced the formation of special tribunals to try people accused of 'killing and torturing fellow Afghans' during the years of the PDPA government.

Afghanistan is entering a dark period of its history; the valiant attempts by communists organised in the PDPA to instigate progressive and democratic reforms has for the moment failed. Whatever faction of the Mojahedin comes out on top in the struggle for power, if any does, will mean death, suffering and poverty for the vast majority of the Afghan people. The reality of imperialism's 'new world order' will be there for all to see in Afghanistan. ∎

PART THREE

Counter-revolution in the Soviet Union 1991

3.1 COMMUNIST PARTY OF THE SOVIET UNION IN DISARRAY
EDDIE ABRAHAMS
FRFI 96 · AUGUST/SEPTEMBER 1990

The 28th Soviet Communist Party Congress, held in July 1990, brought no hope for socialists. It demonstrated that honest communists are a minority in a Party which has ceased to be a coherent instrument of government. It is becoming an arena in which the major trends, none of which are able to fight for the interests of the working class, are battling to defend or win privilege for themselves.

Underlining the possibly unbridgeable gulf that separates the Soviet working class from the Party was the massive 11 July miners' strike. Besides demanding the Ryzkhov government's resignation, the miners concentrated their fire on the Communist Party. They demanded that it cease to organise in workplaces, that its assets be transferred to the state and that it withdraw from all military, educational and security services. Already in some areas, miners have thrown out Communist Party officials from their premises. The sometimes deep hatred for the Party was expressed at rallies where one banner proclaimed 'Long Live the CPSU – in Chernobyl!'.

In addition to Russian working class hostility to the Soviet Communist Party, one must recall that the working class in the smaller Soviet nations in the Baltic, Caucasus and elsewhere has also abandoned the Communist Party for the duplicitous promises of bourgeois nationalists.

As the Party becomes more and more isolated, it is becoming thoroughly demoralised and losing all sense of purpose. Standing currently at 19 million, its membership is falling at an alarming rate. Last year alone 137,000 people resigned. This year the figure will be far higher, especially after the resignations of arch-reactionary Boris Yeltsin and the mayors of Moscow and Leningrad.

In these conditions, it was clear that the Congress could do nothing to resolve the major economic, political and social problems confronting the Soviet Union and its people. The Congress took no major decisions, marked no new turning points, set down no markers for future progress. If it accomplished anything, it was to demonstrate that a substantial section of the misnamed 'conservative' trend (those who proclaim adherence to Marxism–Leninism) had interests as narrow and as selfish as those expressed by the other two major trends in the Party represented by Gorbachev and Yeltsin.

Yegor Ligachev's speech denouncing those who sought to undermine socialism, who rejected its achievements and wanted to introduce private property and restore capitalism, was received with rapturous applause. This contrasted with the reluctant applause extended to Gorbachev and the constant barracking of Leonid Abalkin, an outspoken pro-capitalist deputy Prime Minister. However, when it came to voting, many of those who so warmly applauded Ligachev, endorsed Gorbachev as Party leader and refused to elect Ligachev as deputy leader, choosing instead a pro–Gorbachev hack. These delegates were terrified of a split. Without Gorbachev, the entire Party apparatus, upon which their significant privileges rest, would risk collapse. They preferred Party unity on Gorbachev's own terms to the organisation of a serious struggle against the counter-revolution which is being aided by Gorbachev and spearheaded by the likes of Yeltsin and Abalkin.

As a result Gorbachev was able to conclude the Congress by refashioning the Central Committee to suit his own aims and purposes. Despite the preponderance of 'conservatives', Gorbachev managed to secure the election of outspoken anti-working class elements such as Abalkin and Bunich. Gorbachev and his allies can thus continue to use the CPSU a little while longer.

The lack of an organised socialist current, capable of winning the honest communist among the so-called 'conservatives' and mobilising the working class in determined struggle against the counter-revolution, is a great tragedy for the Soviet working class. It gives imperialism the confidence to proceed unimpeded in its efforts to destroy the last vestiges of the glorious heritage of October 1917. ∎

3.2 GLASNOST AND PERESTROIKA: THE ROAD TO CAPITALIST RESTORATION
EDDIE ABRAHAMS · FRFI 101 · JUNE/JULY 1991

Glasnost (openness – 'democracy') and *perestroika* (economic restructuring were launched by Gorbachev in 1985 in response to the social and economic crisis facing the Soviet Union. Restructuring and democracy were to revive a stagnant economy and society. However, in the absence of an independent working class political force, bourgeois, capitalist counter-revolution seized the initiative.

As a result, the social, economic and political conditions of the overwhelming majority of Soviet people are deteriorating sharply. In the process, and with the aid of the state apparatus, a tiny minority of privileged intellectuals, Party, state and economic functionaries are organising to defend and enlarge their existing privileges by establishing themselves as a new capitalist ruling class.

Despite its enormous size and the fear it inspires among reactionaries the working class is not an independent and determining actor in the drama. Those who are, are fundamentally anti-working class and divided into three main trends: the 'radicals' temporarily grouped around Yeltsin, the so-called 'conservatives' of the CPSU and the forces supporting Gorbachev.

Perestroika

Perestroika has set the foundations for the restoration of capitalism in the USSR with all the main trends supporting the transition to a market economy. They differ only on the speed of the process, some fearing that too rapid a pace will result in uncontrollable working class upheavals.

On 2 April 1991, in the latest manifestation of *perestroika*, food prices went up by an average of 60 per cent. One litre of milk rose from 36 to 50 kopeks. A kilo of beef climbed from two to seven rubles. A 20 kopek loaf now costs 60 kopeks. Overnight Soviet working class living standards dropped. This was the first step of a wider 'anti-crisis' programme designed to ensure a gradual transition to a market economy.

Prime Minister Pavlov predicted that even on this plan the Soviet people should prepare for 18 million unemployed workers and a 20 per cent drop in production. The more 'radical' 'Shatalin' programme which would have entailed 30 million unemployed and a 30 per cent drop in production was rejected last year for fear of the working class response.

Nevertheless the accumulated legal and economic measures of *perestroika* have already set the basis for the development of a new privileged class. Over the past four years, the number of people with an income greater than 250 rubles a month has grown four-fold. 3.1 million people – 2.3 per cent of the workforce – engaged in co-operatives and private business, earn 500 rubles a month, while 500,000 earn 3,000 a month. Meanwhile the average wage remains at 240 rubles; 71 million people, a quarter of the Soviet population, earn less than 100 rubles a month and two million are already unemployed.

A new bourgeoisie is emerging amidst the most blatant corruption and robbery. A Soviet social scientist, Leonid Razikhovskii argues that the economy is today dominated by a 'lumpen-bourgeois ethic' and that it is: 'a unique, historically unprecedented monster – a completely mafia-ized economy.'

An alliance of corrupt party officials, factory managers and private racketeers in the co-operative and growing private sector are ruthlessly plundering the state, illicitly transferring vast resources and funds to the private sector and the black market. Thus while state shops run desperately short, the black market has everything – but at a price beyond the reach of workers.

A Lithuanian government minister stated that:

'... co-operatives and joint enterprises are often oriented not towards the production of consumer goods but towards their redistribution: from the state into their own pockets. If we are to call things by their real names it is speculation on a very large scale.'

Glasnost

Glasnost has benefited the same class which is prospering with perestroika – the so called 'radicals'. They are the privileged intelligentsia – professionals and intellectuals – the 'co-operators' and new entrepreneurs, concentrated in Moscow, Leningrad and the larger cities. Glasnost has enabled them to dominate much of the Soviet press, media, cultural and public political life. Under the pretext of openness and democratic renewal it has allowed them to organise politically and extend their influence.

Virulently anti-socialist and anti-Marxist, they worship every thing capitalist and imperialist. They regard egalitarianism as a 'perversity' and enthusiastically support calls for the rapid introduction of a market economy. They have a virulent hatred for the working class which they fear could bar their selfish ambition. A 'radical' newspaper recently wrote:

'Market reforms begin to be threatened not so much by the machinations of the nomenklatura as by the workers' movement which is gaining momentum spontaneously, and by the radicalisation of the population's sentiments due to price hikes.'

On the margins of this 'radical' camp, glasnost has spawned and given 'freedom' to even more pernicious forces of anti-semitic, proto-fascist Russian chauvinists, monarchists and religious fundamentalists.

Glasnost and the republics

In many national republics the 'radicals' and sections of the party apparatus have coalesced into reactionary pro-capitalist nationalist blocs. Eager to integrate into the world capitalist market they are engaged in a struggle for 'independence' from the USSR.

This is leading to a tragic division and weakening of the Soviet working class and the suppression of national democratic rights. The Georgian government which calls for 'independence' from the Soviet Union is violently crushing the long established Ossetian autonomous region and suppressing the democratic demands of the Mskhetian Turks. In Azerbaijan, the minority Armenian community is subjected to bloody pogroms orchestrated by Azerbaijani 'democratic forces', whilst Armenian 'democratic forces' do the same to the Azeri minority in Armenia. In the Baltic states of Lithuania, Estonia and Latvia, bourgeois nationalist governments have succeeded in whipping up national hostility against the substantial Russian working class, while in massive Russia, Yeltsin who spouts democratic slogans in his fight against Gorbachev, is himself striving to stifle the democratic rights and aspirations of Russia's own 16 autonomous republics, five autonomous regions and ten national districts.

Glasnost, perestroika and foreign policy

The Soviet leadership's foreign policy of accommodating to imperialism has decisively revealed the extent to which it has moved into the camp of counter-revolution. Its full support for the imperialist destruction of Iraq was but the latest and clearest example.

Since the end of the Gulf war the Soviet Foreign Minister visited Israel to prepare for the re-establishment of diplomatic relations. But meetings with the PLO were indefinitely postponed. In the clash between North Korea and the US who are seeking to close down Soviet-built North Korean nuclear reactors, the Soviet

MIKHAIL GORBACHEV

Union is siding with the US. Examples can be multiplied.

The opposition

The main organised political opposition to the Soviet government and the 'radicals' comes from the 'conservatives.' They vocally demand the retention of a united Soviet state and frequently speak out against 'concessions to imperialism'. They do not, however, constitute a working class opposition. They want to retain the Union only because their own power and privilege rests on the gigantic Union-wide economic and military institutions. Whilst willing to see the introduction of the market, they do not, unlike the 'radicals', want Russia to be subordinated to US or European capital. The conservatives have in any event proved themselves too weak, socially isolated and too spineless to influence decisively the direction of events.

Imperialism and the Soviet working class

The imperialists can now rest at ease. The Soviet Union has ceased to represent a threat. Nevertheless they continue to deny credit, financial and technological aid. International capital will do so only when it is sure that private property has been re-established on an unchallenged basis; only when it is confident that its investments will not be endangered by the threat of political and social upheaval and instability.

The corrupt and bureaucratic methods of the CPSU have driven millions of workers to oppose socialism. The working class has been divided, weakened and tainted with nationalism and chauvinism. It nevertheless remains a potential power capable of disrupting the plans of imperialism and its allies in the USSR.

Within the CPSU and outside it, in the factories and mines, there are significant if small groupings of socialists, communists and Marxists who are working hard to politically organise the working class against the tide of reaction. They confront huge problems of ideological confusion, demoralisation and disillusionment but they nevertheless have fertile ground on which to work.

The overwhelming majority of workers oppose the market and the restoration of capitalism. Hatred for private business and co-operatives is widespread. Working class protests demand 'No to free growth of prices!' 'No to the speculators who rob the working people!' 'Shut down all those who gouge the people and steal bread from their mouths.'

A workers' leader summed up working class sentiment:

'The programmes of transition to the market that have been adopted contain within them the danger of violation of the workers' interests. Exploiting the confusion, the administrative-command apparatus is attempting not only to hold onto the reigns of management, but to become in fact the owners of the means of production, creating concerns, associations and joint stock companies. As for us, we are left the role of hired labour, the draught force of the economy. We cannot and simply do not have the right to allow that.' ∎

3.3 AUGUST 1991: COUNTER-REVOLUTION IN THE USSR
EDDIE ABRAHAMS
FRFI 103 · OCTOBER/NOVEMBER 1991

The 19 August 1991 abortive coup attempt in the USSR and the Yeltsin-led counter-coup which it precipitated constituted a crushing victory for bourgeois counter-revolution. By 22 August the stunningly incompetent 'putsch' by the State Emergency Committee was over. Its only function was to have unleashed a furious anti-communist witch-hunt. As mobs dismantled statues of Lenin, Sverdlov and Dzerzhinsky, the CPSU was subjected to a fatal onslaught.

Almost overnight power passed from the CPSU which had ruled the Soviet Union since 1917. The Soviet Communist Party has been more or less demolished. On 24 August Gorbachev resigned as CPSU General Secretary and demanded dissolution of the Central Committee. And by 5 September 1991, the Soviet Union was itself dissolved as the once socialist USSR was transformed into the USS (Union of Sovereign States).

The CPSU meanwhile has been 'suspended' 'pending investigations' into its role in the coup attempt – in fact it played no role. In the Ukraine and the Baltic states it has been banned. Elsewhere its assets have been seized and its newspapers prohibited. Communist Party factory offices have been closed and workplace political organisation forbidden. Thousands of party workers and administrators are being thrown onto the streets.

Despite the fact that the corrupt and careerist-dominated Communist Party apparatus had long ceased to represent the Soviet working class, the campaign against it has nothing to do with opposition to party 'tyranny', 'dictatorship', or 'corruption'. With the dismantling of the entire CPSU, the banning of workplace political organisation and the destruction of statues of the founders of world's first socialist state, it is the heritage of 1917 and working class power which are under attack.

Despite the character of the CPSU, inside it there are hundreds of thousands of workers, including genuine communists, organising to defend the gains of the working class. Within the Soviet industrial and state apparatus tens of thousands of militants are engaged in bitter struggles against corrupt managers and would-be capitalists. The banning of the CPSU is designed primarily to undermine these workers' capacity to organise among the mass of the working class – where opposition to market reforms and privatisation is profound.

In Russia, the largest republic, with 50 per cent of the former USSR's population and 70 per cent of its resources, the Yeltsin camp is now moving to consolidate its political power. The most reactionary anti-working class elements are being rapidly moved into positions of power and privilege as the army, the KGB and the militia are purged and reorganised into anti-working class instruments. Boris Kagarlitsky, a Russian socialist assesses recent developments correctly:

'Yeltsin has announced the triumph of democracy but we have the opposite. We have the end of the democratic intermezzo. We have the transition from the communist dictatorship – which degenerated into democracy – into an anti-communist dictatorship. This anti-communist dictatorship is more dynamic and more capable of suppressing the people.'

The social and political character of the counter-revolution

Against the forces of the Emergency Committee, Yeltsin was able to mobilise the ambitious, pro-capitalist forces of a privileged stratum of professionals, intellectuals and sections of the managerial apparatus of the state and industry. The coup offered them the opportunity of removing the CPSU whose vast bureaucratic apparatus is seen as a competitor in the struggle for power and privilege. With the marginalisation of the CPSU, this layer hopes to extend and secure its own privileges through a rapid transition to capitalism.

The imperialists portrayed Yeltsin and his supporters as people fired by profound democratic and humanitarian ideals. The sordid reality is different. Yeltsin and the social stratum which propelled him to power are inherently and fundamentally anti-democratic. They form part of a parasitic and non-productive section of society which can extend its privileges only at the expense of the working class. They recognise that only capitalism can create conditions where the working class works harder for the benefit of a parasitic minority. This reactionary force therefore wants to dismantle socialism, reverse all socialist gains and destroy independent working class political organisations.

Nikolai Shmelyov, an 'educated' spokesperson for these elements, argues that guaranteed employment is at the root of Soviet economic ills.

'We must also not close our eyes to the economic harm that results from our parasitical certainty of guaranteed employment.'

He believes that 'drunkenness and shoddy workmanship' 'owe much' to 'overemployment' which has transformed Soviet workers into 'a lot of fearless loafers'.

During the Brezhnev years wage differentials between intellectuals

BORIS YELTSIN

and the working class narrowed. Intellectuals are now demanding, in the words of Zaslavskaia, a 'reordering of the wage structure' to restore 'deep' wage differentials between the working class and 'socio-professional groups' who had been 'systematically discriminated against'.

Driven by hatred for egalitarianism and collectivism they perceive socialism as a disease. Soviet society is 'contaminated by an egalitarian psychology and the aggressive rejection of all manifestations of individualism, independence, personal initiative, and the successes which are bound up with this.' Aleksandr Sevastianov believes that socialism has brought about the 'devaluation of intellectual labour' and attacks socialist educational theory claiming that the 'creation of equal conditions for all ran counter to the law of nature.' He wants the dismantling of an educational system founded upon 'romanticised notions about the boundlessness of talent in our people.' Limited talent is, naturally, concentrated among professionals!

Given such a 'democratic' spirit is it surprising that the new powers want to destroy all the achievements of 70 years of socialism?

Why the coup failed

The reactionaries grouped around Yeltsin represent a minority of the population. Nevertheless they overwhelmed the Emergency Committee. The latter, so-called 'conservatives', were thoroughly isolated – socially and politically. Interested primarily in defending their own privileges which were being challenged by the so-called 'radicals', they were incapable of calling upon popular support. There were, and still are, millions of Soviet workers who would happily fight, by any means, to rid themselves of Yeltsin, Gorbachev and other pro-marketeers. But not on behalf of those they perceive as privileged members of a ruling party which does not serve working class interests.

News of the coup was greeted with fleeting hope by many who yearned for the suppression of Gorbachev and Yeltsin. But they rapidly realised that the task was beyond the Emergency Committee. This body's staggering incompetence has invited suspicion that the coup attempt was engineered by an alliance of 'conservatives' and Yeltsinites to impose a strong state during the transition to capitalism.

This committee of 'hardliners' allegedly seeking to restore communist 'tyranny', did not take over communication and transport facilities; allowed railway and metro stations to broadcast Yeltsin's call for a general strike and while arresting Gorbachev did not arrest Yeltsin. The Russian 'White House' which became the focus of resistance did not have its phones or electricity cut off and was open for people to enter or leave at will. And to top it all, the troops and tanks sent into Moscow were, to begin with, unarmed.

In fact the 'hardline communist' coup was a figment of media imagination. Sober bourgeois commentators such as Peregrine Worsthorne understood better:

> 'Renouncing communism is no longer the secret of reform. Even the hardline junta did that. There was no mention of communism throughout its manifesto. Nor is embracing market economics enough. Almost certainly the junta was prepared to do that.'

The Emergency Committee had no progressive programme and no social vision. In fact its social and economic outlook was remarkably like that of Yeltsin's supporters. The Committee was committed to 'support private enterprise'; but it favoured 'urgent' and 'resolute' measures hinting that 'mass manifestations of spontaneous discontent with devastating consequences' were threatened by an uncontrolled imposition of market reforms.

In its foreign policy, the Emergency Committee assured the imperialists that there would be no reverting to 'cold war confrontation' and no resumed support for anti-imperialist movements. Its entire outlook was tainted by a reactionary Great Russian chauvinism. It declared that:

> 'ties [between Soviet nations and peoples] being condemned and severed ... were established on the basis of far broader popular trust which has stood the test of many centuries.'

Given socialism in the USSR was only established this century, the 'many centuries' of 'broad popular trust' refer to the despotic Tsarist oppression of nationalities in its empire!

Capitalist restoration promises poverty, chaos and instability

With the crushing of the coup attempt the entire process of bourgeois restoration will now be accelerated. Imperialist pundits and their Soviet hangers-on are hoping Yeltsin's current popularity will enable him to 'impose protracted economic suffering' on the working class as he takes 'radical' measures to open the country up to imperialist capital. 'Economic reforms' – ie the restoration of private property in production, the impoverishment of the working class for the benefit of a new bourgeoisie – which were delayed by working class opposition will now be foisted upon the country. Whilst the working class will not passively resign itself to 30 million unemployed, hyper-inflation, homelessness and extreme poverty which will be necessary to restore capitalism, the August counter-revolution has made capital's task that much easier.

The Russian Republic has now emerged as the major force in the region. In the face of its power and wealth, pretensions to national independence by the other republics will soon be moderated and tempered. The Russian government has already unleashed its mighty whip warning its neighbouring Asiatic republics not to go for total independence on pain of losing slices of Russian-populated territory to the Russian Republic. Meanwhile in the smaller republics, nationalist governments are preparing pogroms against minorities and against each other. As the disintegration of the USSR continues apace, it is the working class and poor who will pay with their blood and lives, as aspiring bourgeois factions prepare, even by war, to seize a share of the new capitalist paradise.

Political disintegration is being accompanied by devastating economic collapse. Before the coup, then Deputy Prime Minister, Vladimir Shcherbakov warned of famine in the Soviet Union. This year's grain harvest is expected to drop to 195-200 million tonnes. Edward Shevardnadze, former Gorbachev Foreign Minister warned that 'people could take to the streets', creating a crisis which could be exploited by 'dangerous people', meaning of course workers fighting for their rights. Soviet economists are also predicting hyper-inflation by the year's end. In 1988 the state printed 11.5 billion rubles. By August 1991, 150 billion had already been printed. Production levels are set to fall by a massive 15 to 20 per cent this year.

Imperialism, allied with Gorbachev, had hoped to secure a stable transition to capitalism in the USSR. Today, with Gorbachev much diminished and Yeltsin ascendant, it is confronted with the prospect of a disintegrating cauldron of national, economic, social and political forces. As economic crisis and political conflict sharpen, the entire area could explode into chaos, violence and even war. The disintegration of Yugoslavia, in comparison, could appear benign. Imperialism will nevertheless negotiate and respond to these problems from a position of greater self-confidence and arrogance. For they have laid low the greatest challenge so far to capitalism – the Bolshevik Revolution of 1917. ∎

3.4 RUSSIA: YELTSIN'S NEW AUTOCRACY
EDDIE ABRAHAMS
FRFI 104 · DECEMBER/JANUARY 1991/92

In November 1991, for the first time since 1917, there was no official commemoration of the October Bolshevik Revolution in what was once the Soviet Union. Nevertheless, despite severe anti-communist repression, several thousand communists and socialists gathered in Moscow's main square to defend the heritage of 1917. Their target was the Yeltsin government and among their slogans was 'Down with the Dictatorship of the Bourgeoisie'.

A month or two ago the British left, which applauded the Yeltsin counter-revolution, would have dismissed such slogans as expressions of outlandish Stalinist frustration. But today there is nothing to cover up the reactionary character of Yeltsin's counter-coup. We are witnessing the establishment not of 'democracy', but bourgeois rule in its most anti–working class and anti–democratic form. Russian socialist Boris Kagarlitsky, who is by no means an adherent of the Bolshevik tradition, argues that: 'This is not just a restoration of capitalism, but the restoration of the old (autocratic) pre–February 1917 regime.' The Russian working class will be the main target for this revived autocracy.

Yeltsin's model of democracy

Russian President Yeltsin is concentrating all power in his own hands and rules more or less by decree. Decree No. 96, for example, deprived the elected Moscow Soviet of most of its constitutional powers. While in Moscow and Leningrad executives usurp the powers of elected soviets, elsewhere Yeltsin has dispatched appointed governors to take control of every region and autonomous republic. Equally ominously, the government has established a new National Guard with wages of about five times the average worker's earnings!

On 1 November, the Russian parliament overwhelmingly backed proposals to ban, for the foreseeable future, all referenda and almost all elections in Russia. Following the August counter-coup the Communist Party was 'suspended' pending an 'investigation'. Yeltsin has replaced this with a decree banning the Party and confiscating its property! Russian socialists believe his next effort will be the dismantling of the official trade unions on the grounds that they were associated with the now illegal Communist Party. With their massive apparatus and membership, and their own printing presses and newspapers, these unions could become formidable obstacles to capitalist restoration.

Such are the preparations being made by Russia's new 'democratic' government to cope with the inevitable working class resistance to Yeltsin's 'radical' economic reforms, which were also overwhelmingly carried by the Russian parliament. These propose a rapid, Polish–style, privatisation of state assets and an end to all subsidies and price controls. These 'reforms' will generate massive poverty and 40 million unemployed people. They will demolish all the social, economic and political gains made by the working class since 1917.

Such steps, directed against the majority, against the working class, and necessary for the restoration of capitalism, cannot be secured by democratic means. The pro-capitalist 'democrats' who support Yeltsin understand this. An *Isvetzia* supplement recently noted:

'Yes in Russia we need a harsh, and in many ways authoritarian government. The President of Russia will soon have to confront that which is more dangerous than any elite junta – unemployment, the immiseration of millions of people. Destructive strikes are inevitable and explosions of violence are possible. In these circumstances it will be necessary to do unpleasant things – to forbid, to maybe even disperse, to introduce order.'

Those who suggested a Swedish social democratic model for the Soviet transition to capitalism are ignorant of the relationship between politics and economics. With a foreign debt of more than $60 billion, with industrial output likely to collapse by 20 per cent this year on top of a budget deficit of 300 billion rubles, the Russian economy is too weak to sustain a stable bourgeois democratic order. Thus Yeltsin is building the foundations for a bourgeois autocracy!

Reactionary nationalism abroad

The economic collapse and political disintegration of the ex-USSR has also set the scene for reactionary nationalist conflict. The aspirant bourgeoisie of the 16 ex-Soviet republics are all eager to lay their hands on the largest slice of the disintegrated USSR's assets. Yeltsin's Russian government, however, has clarified its position. Anatoly Sobchak, the Mayor of Leningrad announced: 'Russia will be dictating to the Republics and not vice versa. This is what they have to realise.'

Within Russia this dictatorship takes the form of banning referenda on independence in Russia's own 16 autonomous regions. If such a diktat is defied, as in Checheno-Ingushetia, the curfew and state of emergency is invoked. For the former Soviet republics, the forum for dictatorship is the new Economic Union established by Yeltsin and

Gorbachev. Most republics, too weak to resist, have signed up.

But not the Ukraine. Producing 46 per cent of Soviet agriculture and 25 per cent of its coal and possessing significant industry, the aspirant Ukrainian bourgeoisie wants to go it alone. It plans to set up its own currency, retain control of nuclear weapons on its territory and form an army of 400,000. With Russia determined to retain real control of these resources, this struggle will become more bitter and dangerous.

The new Russian left

The working class is the only force capable of resisting the economic disintegration, political instability and nationalist warfare which now grips Yeltsin's Russia and the ex-Soviet Union. With winter coming, millions of ordinary people are beginning to realise that Yeltsin, far from solving their economic problems, is in fact making them worse. On 23 October 1991, the first substantial workers' demonstration of 40,000 people took place in Moscow against 'economic reforms'. Such opposition will be limited and largely inefficient so long as the working class does not have its own political organisations. To rebuild such organisations is the task set themselves by a number of Russian socialist forces.

The *Initiating Group for the Association of Russian Left Forces of Socialist Orientation* wants to create a 'new party' on 'the basis of the progressive forces of the CPSU'. It notes that 'the CPSU . . . has exhausted itself, has lost trust, and has in fact ceased its existence.' The co-ordinators of another proposed *Russian Party of Labour* intend to create 'an authentic left movement' which 'gives political support to the trade union and the workers movement.'

These are among the many groupings trying to reconstruct a movement that defends and advances on the positive achievements of the past 70 years – free education, health care, the right to full employment, housing rights and the whole system of social guarantees. They all see the new order in Russia as fundamentally detrimental to the interests of the working class. Their immediate task is the defence of the official trade unions. Boris Kagarlitsky explains: 'If the government smashes the unions we have today, we will have no time or possibility to build new ones. There would be no unions to protect the workers.'

The political character, the traditions, ideology and outlook of many of these forces are not yet clear. Many are hostile to Marxism and the Bolshevik tradition as they understand them. Many oppose longstanding concepts within the communist movement – the vanguard party, the dictatorship of the proletariat etc. Some even applaud the Menshevik tradition. But nothing is yet settled. Communists elsewhere would be irresponsible sectarians if they dismissed these forces. In the current political confusion and turmoil and in totally new conditions, no revolutionary movement will emerge overnight. The decisive thing is that these forces are striving to organise the working class politically against the devastation promised by the new order. The bitter struggles which will accompany such work will sort out and clarify the ideological and political outlook of a new Russian socialist movement. ■

3.5 WHO IS BORIS YELTSIN?
MAXINE WILLIAMS
FRFI 103 · OCTOBER/NOVEMBER 1991

Boris Yeltsin is the West's man of the moment. But bourgeois politicians do not like unknown quantities. Specifically, they feel uncomfortable with populist politicians who have, however fraudulently, established a link with masses of people. Hence the plethora of articles attempting to understand Yeltsin. Will he take the unimaginably harsh measures that the reimposition of capitalism in the Soviet Union will require? Will he, if it comes to it, pass the true test of a bourgeois democrat and shoot the workers in the streets?

Yeltsin the bully has already been on display in his humiliation of Gorbachev, his threats to the non-Russian republics and his amassing of previously all-Union powers into his own hands. What will he do next?

His autobiography, *Against the Grain* offers some insight into the man. Most autobiographies are self-serving, but Yeltsin's is crudely so. Its tone is the relentless 'I'm no intellectual. I'm a basic, honest chap but I know what's what' much beloved by right-wing British trade union leaders.

'When analysing situations and events, I ignore whatever went well and concentrate on my shortcomings and mistakes. This is one of the basic traits of my character. I don't know whether it is good or bad.'

'At school I stood out from my classmates by my energy and drive.'

'My main arguments in the battle for discipline were my own total dedication to the job.'

'There began a period of furious activity and, as always, I spared myself less than anyone.'

This tone persists throughout. The cumulative effect is singularly repellent. This man's lack of any clearly expressed political principle, alongside his egomania, should make one fear for the future of those he now leads.

And what are his ideological beliefs?

'I am in favour of the creation of National Fronts, but only on condition that their programmes and actions do not run counter to accepted human values.'

Here is a thing. What are 'accepted human values'? Clearly in the Soviet Union of 1991 'accepted human values' are in short supply, especially in nationalist circles. Most ominously, given the history of Tsarist Russian expansionism, deeply embedded Russian chauvinism has again surfaced. Yeltsin has not only refused to counter this but with his threats to alter borders, is the embodiment of such views.

Aside from his 'human values', what does Yeltsin think?

Under Reagan, 'major improvements, especially in the American economy were there for all to see'. Obviously Yeltsin has not heard of the plight of the millions of poor in the USA. When he visited the USA he met with representatives of the Cuban-American community and promised them he would cut off aid to Cuba. Today, he is keen to inflict

Reagonomics on the Soviet people: 'A quite different prospect was offered to us by the promised democratisation of society, in which individual interest and individual responsibility would be paramount, to which should be added a withdrawal of state subsidies from industry . . . ' Yeltsin appears to have no care at all about the catastrophic effect of such actions – tens of millions would be unemployed overnight. He is, of course, for private ownership of property, including land and no limits on private enterprise.

Yeltsin's contribution to the struggle against privilege was, as he proudly boasts, to belatedly refuse his right to get food from Party shops and instead . . . to send his wife out queueing for two hours a day. He instinctively knows what a bourgeois politician means when he talks of 'sacrifice'!

He spits out venom on even the idea of socialism:

'We shall soon realise that we are practically the only country left on earth which is trying to enter the 21st century with an obsolete 19th-century ideology; that we are the last inhabitants of a country defeated by socialism . . . '

The real question is how such a man, whose ideological partner is Thatcher, could not only have risen so far in a 'Communist Party', but could finally have defeated it.   ■

3.6 IMPERIALISM CONSOLIDATES COUNTER-REVOLUTION
EDDIE ABRAHAMS
FRFI 106 · APRIL/MAY 1992

The catastrophic economic, political and social disintegration in Russia and the other republics of the Commonwealth of Independent States (CIS) has finally spurred the Group of Seven imperialist powers to launch a $24 billion aid programme. Consisting of $18 billion in credits and loan guarantees and a further $6 billion to help stabilise the ruble, the package is designed in the first instance to stem growing political opposition to the IMF-imposed 'reform programme' and control the pace of disintegration of the old socialist economy.

The imperialist powers now realise that without external aid, the economic and social collapse in the CIS could rapidly and severely undermine European economic and political stability. They are also worried by the prospect of a potentially massive opposition to capitalist restoration. Indeed just before the announcement a group of imperialist 'experts' predicted a massive social explosion unless the pace of reform was slackened. Thus President Bush declared the package to be 'a comprehensive and integrated programme to support the struggle for freedom', and German Chancellor Kohl explained that the 'West must do everything possible to contribute towards the stabilisation of the democracy and the economy there.'

Through this programme, combining the efforts of the IMF ($4 billion), the World Bank ($1.5 billion) as well as the European Bank for Reconstruction and Development, export credit guarantees and food credits, the Group of Seven hopes irrevocably to bind Russia and the CIS, as subordinate, Third World, elements, into the imperialist/ capitalist market. As a by-product, they hope that the resulting increased international trade and production will play a role in helping to push their own economies out of recession. The programme is clearly not designed to reconstruct and revive the CIS economies along 'European' lines. Such a programme would cost anything between $80–160 billion. The imperialists are happy to spend such sums on arms, not on the ex-socialist bloc!

The Group of Seven has made it clear that humanitarian considerations play no part in their calculations. An 'absolute precondition' for aid is that the CIS accept IMF 'adjustment programmes'. This will amount to an unprecedented attack on working class living standards and conditions. In the IMF-orchestrated transition to market economy, the old centrally planned economy, the foundation of guaranteed employment and social provision, is being systematically destroyed. For the working class Latin American poverty, not Swedish-style affluence has finally arrived.

At the beginning of January, in a first major step towards the capitalist market, the Russian government freed most prices of goods and services from state control. Immediately average prices shot up by between 250 per cent and 700 per cent as monopoly hoarders, speculators and merchants prepared to make massive profits. Overnight, 80 per cent of Russia's 150 million population was pushed below the government's poverty line as even subsistence goods were priced out of reach. In order to preempt working class resistance the government doubled wages to 750 rubles. Yet even on official calculations an average family needs 1,300 rubles to rise above the poverty line. In true capitalist fashion, Russia's Minister for Economy urged workers to 'restrain wage demands' in the interests of fighting hyperinflation!

Mass unemployment is also about to hit the working class. IMF-imposed reforms will withdraw subsidies from and privatise services, agriculture and industry. The result will be devastating. Hitherto affecting mainly women and civil servants, the International Labour Organisation predicts that by the end of 1992 unemployment could reach 15 million for the whole of the CIS. A further 30 million workers are threatened with imminent redundancy. They are so severely underemployed as to be effectively without work. The same report notes that of the 500,000 so far registered unemployed, a mere 16 per cent receive benefits. The figure for the USA, which does not even have a welfare state, is 34 per cent! The government is nevertheless planning to cut unemployment pay, regarding present levels as too generous.

Imperialism, through the IMF, is dictating terms which will make the position worse. By the end of June 1992 all remaining price controls will be lifted and a massive 28 per cent VAT on most goods will be restored. This measure was initially withdrawn for fear of popular protest. In addition, as with Third World countries, the IMF is demanding that Russia's budget deficit be reduced to

MOSCOW BARRICADES, 1991

101

one per cent of GNP. This means further drastic cuts in all subsidies to education, health, welfare, housing and cultural work.

These 'economic reforms' are destroying the productive and administrative apparatus of the old centrally planned economy. A report from the Institute of International Finance notes that:

'The breakdown of a unified administrative structure will disrupt traditional trade flows . . . shortages of material inputs are likely to intensify. Real net material product (NMP) may fall another 15 per cent in Russia . . . and output may fall . . . by more than a quarter in several republics.'

In 1992 oil production is likely to drop by 14 per cent from last year's depleted levels, iron and steel by 15 per cent, chemicals by 16 per cent and food products by 18 per cent. In January alone, retail trade, measured in physical terms, fell by 63 per cent, processed milk for sale on the market by 46 per cent and tractor production by 49 per cent. These statistics of collapse spell greater misery for the working class. For the first time in generations Russia is seeing queues for bread.

Economic collapse is compounded by the disintegration of effective government. With no effective fiscal administration billions of rubles are being lost to tax evaders and other thieves. The government's weakness and lack of grip is revealed in remarks by academician Georgi Arbatov. He claims that the Russian government is:

'. . . the most disorganised . . . They don't answer letters, don't reply to phone calls on the special line; they don't carry out their commitments . . . in the new structure of power corruption is practically legalised and without limit.'

This state of affairs is by no means deplored by all. This, after all, is the form taken by the transition to capitalism and the emergence of a ruling class. While the majority are hurled into poverty, a tiny minority of unbridled and selfish bourgeois aspirants, working with the IMF, imperialist advisors, banks and companies are hoping to accumulate capital through speculation, theft and corruption of all sorts. It is they who will benefit from the Group of Seven aid package, not the working class.

While the economy collapses and millions face hunger, Russia's new 'entrepreneurs' are hoarding nearly $15 billion of desperately needed hard currency in overseas banks. For a large kickback they are planning to sell off the ex-Soviet Union's largest enterprises in oil, gas, telecommunications and car sectors to imperialist firms. Meanwhile, they are simply distributing among themselves huge chunks of state property and land!

The Yeltsin government does not exist to fashion a 'new democratic order' for the Russian people. It is an agent not of renewal but of the Latin Americanisation of the former USSR. The current Russian government is proposing to return to a handful of private owners the means of production which belong to the Russian people, and transform workers once more into wage slaves and serfs to capital. Throughout Russia and the CIS a new layer of greedy, narrow minded and selfish millionaires is now flourishing. They lack any principles or ideals besides making money at the expense of public property. They do not care what happens to their republics or the masses so long as they themselves make money.

However, their consolidation of political, economic and social power is not taking place without potentially explosive contradictions. The collapse of the economy and the diminishing national product has led to severe clashes for control of land, property and wealth by the differing factions of the aspirant bourgeoisie. This is expressed in intense nationalist rivalries ranging from bloody military clashes in the Caucasus to the, for the moment, virulent political contest between Russia and the Ukraine. Even Russia is threatened with disintegration as the leadership of its 20 autonomous regions bid for control of immensely profitable oil, gas, diamond, gold and other resources.

Meanwhile, the extreme polarisation of wealth and poverty could precipitate massive social upheaval and a sustained working class opposition to the introduction of market forces. Already, there are weekly protests against the Yeltsin government in almost every major town across Russia. In February, fearful of a miners' strike, the government trebled their wages only to be confronted with demands for similar rises by bus drivers and teachers. Popular discontent is providing fertile ground for the organised political opposition which includes, besides communist and social democratic forces, some outright fascist and anti-Semitic elements.

In a struggle against the working class, the new regime is by no means assured of victory. Its governmental writ does not run far and its state apparatus and machinery of repression is at the moment weak and relatively ineffective. Revealing of the new state's weakness was a comment by Alexander Shokin, a Deputy Prime Minister and Minister of Labour:

> 'The gap between the federal structures and the local level is very wide. We can issue any number of decrees but it is very difficult to implement them on a local level.'

The armed forces inherited from the old regime are unreliable and in a process of disintegration. General Samsonov, Chief of Staff of CIS forces, speaking of desertions and draft evasion said:

> 'The situation has arisen where we can no longer defend ourselves. There is no one left. There are units in which officers have to stand guard. It is shameful.'

Solving this problem is the Yeltsin government's priority task. They are aware that democratic rights for the working class are not compatible with a process of capitalist restoration in which the majority of the working class is impoverished. They have noted that trade unions, left-wing opposition and the working class generally are already using the limited democratic rights available to oppose the brazen theft and robbery by the new elite. Increasingly, therefore, voices are heard demanding a Pinochet-style dictatorship. Only recently, Russian Minister of Security, Vicktor Barannikov noted:

> 'The only real force that can defend the reform in Russia is the armed forces and our apparatus. The people are sick of *perestroika*. Only armed detachments can guarantee the success of reforms.'

Speaking of the Russian parliament where the opposition is growing stronger, Barannikov said:

'These are good for nothings. They should be dispersed.'

To this end Yeltsin is trying to consolidate a new militia and an officer corps. He has doubled the officers' salaries and offered them extensive benefits and privileges. Simultaneously, the Yeltsin government is strengthening its elite 'anti-corruption/crime' force OMON which was used against a communist war veterans' demonstration on 23 February. Despite the problems which beset it, the new regime remains immensely powerful. It has control of financial resources, it controls the media and has the means to develop a repressive apparatus. But, most crucially, it has the backing of imperialism which can when necessary temporarily buy off sections who are moving into opposition to 'reform'.

The working class movement confronts incredible difficulties and will have to make complicated political decisions as it organises to resist capitalist restoration. The organised left-wing opposition is small and divided into numerous, constantly changing organisations. Among them, *Trudoyava Rossiya* groups the *All Union of Bolsheviks* (followers of Stalin and Brezhnev), the *Russian Communist Workers Party* (a Marxist-Leninist grouping but not 'Stalinist') and the *Communist Union*. Another bloc unites the *Socialist Party of Working People*, led by ex-CPSU member Roy Medvedev, the *Russian Party of Labour* and the *Russian Party of Communists*. Inheriting all the accumulated discredit of the past these forces are at the moment relatively isolated. But if they succeed in uniting on a common platform in defence of the working class, they could present a formidable obstacle to capitalist restoration.   ∎

PART FOUR

Cuba resists!

4.1 CASTRO DEFENDS THE CUBAN REVOLUTION
DAVID REED
FRFI 95 · JUNE/JULY 1990

Over the last few months, following the counter-revolutionary developments in Eastern Europe, the imperialists have been counting the days to the fall of the Cuban Revolution. Like hovering vultures they eagerly speculate on the downfall of Fidel Castro. Communism, they believe, will be finally laid to rest with the destruction of the Cuban Revolution.

The imperialists have employed battalions of journalists to spread the message of Cuba's imminent collapse. Fidel Castro realises that this widespread propaganda against himself and the Cuban Revolution is part of the ideological assault on Marxism-Leninism and communism and has to be politically countered. In the last few months, in a series of important interviews and speeches, he has taken this assault head on and given clear political answers to the most vital issues raised. They have been translated and printed in recent issues of the Cuban national newspaper *Granma* (in March and April 1990) and are essential reading for any communist in this country. Below is a summary with edited extracts of some of his views on the prospects for the Cuban Revolution and for socialism generally in the wake of recent international developments, in Eastern Europe and Central and Latin America.

Counter-revolution in Eastern Europe

Castro has made it plain that the European socialist community has collapsed and the restoration of capitalism is underway in most of the countries of Eastern Europe. This has already had an economic impact on Cuba. Trade agreements have not been renewed and with the privatisation and closure of industrial enterprises, for example the Ikarus bus factory in Hungary, industrial goods and spare parts are no longer available. As a result, in assessing the immediate impact on Cuba, Fidel Castro has felt free to speak about the quality of the goods received from these countries.

'The truth is as follows: we are exporters of foodstuffs and raw materials . . . so necessary for industrial development of any kind. We don't export trash . . . and often what we get in return is junk . . . there is some junk that only we buy and nevertheless we make it function, because we specialise in that after so many years: taking rubbish and trying to make something useful out of it.'

He gives the example of Bulgarian forklifts. Cuba was the only country in the world which bought them. 'There are hundreds, even thousands of these forklifts standing idle in our warehouses.' They have to improvise to get them to work, seeing which parts are useful and obtaining other parts elsewhere or making them in Cuba. Similarly Hungarian buses with their Czech gearboxes are appalling. They get 'six kilometres per gallon and fill the city with exhaust fumes poisoning everybody.' Now Cuba is making its own bus which achieves 11 kilometres per gallon and, having a much better engine, causes less pollution.

This is, nevertheless, a very serious situation for Cuba. Castro compares it to the early years of the Revolution, when the United States imposed its blockade:

'. . . there weren't any spare parts for our machinery, for our equipment, for our factories, for anything. We must confront that same situation now, except now it's on account of the attitude of those Eastern European countries which have joined with the United States of America.'

107

He says he is not sure what the Eastern European countries will get for doing this but believes they will soon see some reward for taking the side of the empire in the form of World Bank or IMF credits or most favoured nation status. This has already influenced these countries' political attitudes, as demonstrated by a recent vote at the United Nations on a US-sponsored anti-Cuban motion on human rights in Cuba.

'Poland and Czechoslovakia, yoked like oxen to Panama, co-sponsored the US motion together with NATO. They didn't even have to vote on it; they did it for free.'

They were joined by two other countries previously in the socialist camp, Hungary and Bulgaria. Castro drives home the significance of this:

'Just look, what a change, what gains, what progress, what great "revolutionary" reforms they have made, in order to end up right in the lap of US imperialism and plot against the revolutionary movement. This is the negation of everything that has been progressive in the world . . . for countries which until yesterday were allegedly socialist to do this now along with the US imperialists, the enemy of humanity, the oppressor of our peoples . . . What decency remains in those countries? What is left of socialism? . . . What can be left with this repugnant behaviour?'

Castro says that, with the changes in Europe, the imperialist countries want to turn the former socialist countries into new capitalist countries which will participate in the plunder of the Third World. He says it will not be easy and without conflict.

' . . . It won't be easy because it will take time for capitalism there to develop the efficiency it has in the First World; this is because among other things, in order to build capitalism you not only need capital, you need capitalists, businessmen, and they don't have them.'

In Poland this has already led to conflicts between Walesa and the

Polish Prime Minister and to splits in Solidarity, with Solidarity 80 charging: 'Walesa and the government with having implemented austerity policies that are unbearable for the people, whose real income has been cut by half.' It remains to be seen what will happen but, for the present, Castro says, the leaders of Poland, Czechoslovakia, Hungary and Bulgaria have clarified our ideas and revolutionary understanding:

> 'They have made us feel, if possible, more revolutionary, more socialist, more Marxist-Leninist, more loyal to Marti . . . We feel even more repugnance for those in the international movement who have signed a pact with imperialism. All this teaches us a lesson, it deepens our convictions and makes us stauncher and more resolute.'

The Soviet Union and Cuba

The USSR has resisted pressures from US imperialism to hold back trade with Cuba as was shown by the recent delivery of some Mig-29 fighters. This agreement was signed five years ago and more aircraft will be delivered during 1990. While there are obviously major economic problems facing the Soviet Union, which, at times, will mean delays, and other difficulties in goods and raw material deliveries, Castro believes, in the present circumstances, that the Soviet Union intends to fulfil its trade agreements with Cuba.

Castro argues that the situation in the Soviet Union is different from that in Eastern Europe.

The Soviet Union hasn't fallen into the hands of counter-revolutionaries, and we hope it won't. The Soviet Union hasn't disintegrated and we hope it won't. No civil war has broken out in the Soviet Union

FIDEL CASTRO

109

and we hope it won't – yet dangers, real dangers, are lurking.'

So Cuba is preparing for this eventuality and would adopt measures, a 'special period', which would mean a halt to all social development programmes for a number of years, in order to ensure some overall economic development and continue the food programme.

The survival of the Cuban Revolution

US imperialism is intent on destroying the Cuban Revolution. Recent developments in Nicaragua and Panama show its determination to destroy any regime which stands in its way. A recent US provocation against Cuba is an attempt to broadcast anti-Cuban programmes to Cuba through TV Marti by pirating a Cuban-designated TV frequency. The name of the station is a calculated insult to Cuba, equivalent, Castro argues, to finding a brothel somewhere and calling it George Washington. The US leadership are imbeciles because the effect is to create a more solid union in Cuban society and greater hatred of the United States government. Cuban technicians have completely jammed the TV broadcasts leaving the US government looking very stupid.

Many people have suggested to Castro that he should make concessions to US imperialism and that the present stance of Cuba is suicidal. His reply is unequivocal:

'What right does imperialism have to tell us what we must do, what socio-economic system we must develop, what political and electoral methods to use? . . . those who think they can survive by making concessions to the enemy are lost; only the brave survive, those who resist, those who struggle.'

The US invasion of Panama has had an impact on the Cuban people. It has served to broaden their political culture and their hatred for injustice, arrogance and aggression by the United States. So has the dirty war waged by US imperialism against Nicaragua. Nor can the situation in Cuba be compared to that in Eastern Europe:

'Don't you think that disaster will teach our people that revolutions must be genuine and made by each people; that revolution cannot be imported or exported? That a revolution as profound as that of socialism, which came into being for the first time after thousands of years of human civilisation and clashes with much of our individualism, selfishness etc, etc, in order to be solid and invincible must also be genuine? Our revolution wasn't a gift from anybody, it wasn't sent by anybody, it wasn't borrowed from anybody, it wasn't imported from anywhere, we made it our-selves. That's why it can't be confused with any other political process elsewhere.'

Given these circumstances, Castro believes that in the face of US aggression not only will the Cuban people resist but they will win. 'The price of a US attack on Cuba would be so high that it would be unpayable'.

'Whenever they wage an inglorious little war they get applause, the Grenada invasion, the Panama invasion, but then as soon as they start receiving coffins with the bodies of the invaders, the euphoria is over, the applause is over and the tears begin to be shed.'

Castro reminds us of Vietnam. The Vietnamese had to pay a high price but they fought and defended themselves and the US had to withdraw. 'For many years we have prepared our people to resist even in the case of total occupation.' They are prepared not just to resist but to win.

Imperialism is sitting on a volcano

Castro admits that the position of the imperialist countries looks good in economic terms. But their wealth and opulence is based on the plunder of oppressed peoples. Castro doubts whether this situation can be maintained much longer given the social and economic situation of Third World countries. In Latin America, illiteracy and poverty are growing, economic growth is negligible and with inflation rates overall of 1,000 per cent the situation is now uncontrollable. The imperialist countries are 'sitting on a volcano which can erupt. That volcano is in the Third World and nobody has an answer for these problems. Capitalism won't solve these problems.' Socialism can.

' . . . In 30 years of socialist Revolution we have solved what Latin America hasn't solved in 200 years. The education levels of our people are greater than those of the United States; our health indices are similar to those of the United States . . . The capital of the United States, the capital of the empire has an infant mortality rate in the first year of life three times greater than in Havana . . . '

The volcano is there waiting to erupt. It is in the Third World countries. Castro believes that the overconfidence of the imperialists 'will only be a passing feeling and people will react. The world revolutionary and progressive forces will raise their heads and regain their morale.' Until that time we can be certain that Fidel Castro and the Cuban people will uphold and defend the revolutionary banner of socialism, of Marxism-Leninism, no matter what happens and in all circumstances. As communists our task is to fight alongside them. ∎

4.2 INTERNATIONALISM MEANS SAVING THE CUBAN REVOLUTION
DAVID REED
FRFI 98 · DECEMBER/JANUARY 1990/91

The Cuban Revolution is facing one of the greatest tests in its nearly 32 year history. Many of Cuba's economic and development plans have been severely set back following the growing disintegration of the Soviet Union and the collapse of the East European socialist bloc. On top of this has come the rapid escalation in the price of oil resulting from the Gulf crisis. Compounding these problems is the ever present and ever more rigorous US blockade of the country.

To defend the Revolution, and therefore socialism, Cuba has been forced to enter a 'special period' – a national economic emergency to ensure its economic and political survival. The defence of the Cuban revolution is of prime concern to communists everywhere for it is intimately bound up with the defence of Marxism-Leninism and the communist standpoint. In these difficult times for communists it has fallen on the Cuban people to be the standard-bearers of revolutionary ideas, to defend them in practice by ensuring the survival of their Revolution.

The economic setbacks and the inevitable hardship forced on the Cuban people offer fertile ground for dissident and counter-revolutionary groups to organise against the Revolution. Undoubtedly US imperialism will seize every opportunity to sustain and promote these groups as it tightens its economic blockade against Cuba. To confront these problems the Cuban Communist Party, far from retreating as Communist Parties have done elsewhere, is conducting an unrelenting ideological struggle in defence of socialism and socialist principles. By pointing to the just and admirable forms of economic co-operation which existed between Cuba and the Soviet Union, by showing the superiority of socialist methods of confronting the present crisis, Castro is conducting an ideological struggle not only to win over the Cuban people but also to build support for socialist Cuba and for socialism among the peoples of Latin America and the Third World.

The Soviet Union and Cuba

While asserting the independence of the Cuban Revolution, 'nobody made it for us, nobody defended it for us, nobody saved it for us', Castro points to the political and economic importance of Cuba's relation to the Soviet Union. That the October Revolution took place was 'a privilege, a stroke of good fortune . . . for our Revolution'. In the days when some people want to smash statues of Lenin into pieces, 'we feel the figure of Lenin growing in our hearts and our thoughts.' He reminds people of Lenin's historical significance:

> 'Lenin's work has endured throughout history and has helped to change the world. Lenin's work meant the emergence of the first socialist state in human history, and this state saved humanity from fascism . . . The first socialist state meant an advance for the peoples' liberation movements and the end of colonialism, and it

meant so much to us when the imperialists wanted to destroy our Revolution, when they blockaded us and tried to starve us out.'

Political and economic relations were established between Cuba and the Soviet Union based on new and admirable forms of co-operation 'which signified the end of unequal terms of trade'. Never before was there more justice in the economic relations between industrialised and underdeveloped countries. On that basis Cuban factories were built, agriculture was developed and mechanised and electrification extended throughout the country. On that basis five-year plans between Cuba and the Soviet Union and the other socialist countries were worked out.

When, in a very short period of time, the socialist camp disappeared, Cuba 'abruptly lost the pillars of its economic agreements with many of those countries of the socialist camp'. The Soviet Union 'remains' but it is going through a profound political, economic and social crisis and, because it is the strongest pillar of Cuba's economic and social development, this crisis is having a dramatic impact on Cuba's economy.

The construction of a nuclear power plant built with the help of the Soviet Union has fallen behind. They do not know when it will be ready or whether it will be finished. The Moa nickel plant has been shut down because of shortage of fuel. A recently finished oil refinery cannot be started up because of lack of fuel. There is already a deficit in fuel supplies from the Soviet Union of two million tons as well as major deficits in industrial raw materials including fertilisers which play a vital role in the Cuban economy.

The Soviet government has, however, made great efforts to meet its commitments. It has ignored the threats of the United States which has attempted to make the cessation of Soviet economic co-operation with Cuba the condition for improved Soviet-US relations. Although there are some in the USSR who would put an end to the co-operative relations with Cuba to 'get in good with the empire' that is not the position of the Soviet government. However at the present time no one knows what the basis of Cuba's trade with the Soviet Union is going to be next year: what the Soviet Union will pay for Cuban sugar and other products, what price Cuba will pay for Soviet products and how much fuel will be available.

Oil and the Gulf crisis

The Gulf crisis has aggravated the problems associated with shortages of oil. It has become a world tragedy especially for Cuba. The price of oil before the crisis was about $14 a barrel; it has now reached $40. Trade would be unworkable if Cuba were charged the going price for oil and paid rock bottom prices for its sugar, which is the price called for on the world market but which does not exist anywhere. For example, in trading relations between the European Community nations prices paid for sugar are above the so-called world market price even if there is excess supply.

Cuba consumes some 13 million tons of oil. If war breaks out in the Gulf and the oil price reaches $50-60 a barrel, then, at the current world market price for sugar, Cuba would need some 26 million tons of sugar to acquire 13 million tons of oil. That is an amount in the region of all the sugar sold in the world. With the present price of $40 a barrel Cuba would require some 18 million tons of sugar.

At the time of the Cuban Revolution the price of oil was $2 a barrel. With less than a million tons of sugar Cuba could purchase all the oil the country consumed. In the intervening period the price of oil has increased nearly 20 times, while sugar prices have remained rock bottom. The imperialists are complaining that the Soviet Union pays Cuba too high a price for its sugar but it is oil that has been and is more overpriced than sugar. Sugar is sold to the Soviet Union at a price more or less equivalent to the cost of producing a ton of sugar in the USSR and sometimes cheaper. The price at which Cuba has been buying oil in the past years is far higher than the cost of producing it. 'In truth, oil is one of the most privileged and overpriced products in the world – priced many times higher than the cost of production.'

This is an expression of the difficulties facing Cuba, and Castro believes they could still get much worse.

Cuba confronts the 'special period'

If Cuba is to confront a 'special period' in peace time its task must be not just one of survival but also of development. While rationing and shortages of key products are inevitable, the country's basic development programmes such as the food programme would have to be maintained. This means going ahead with the application of science and technology to agriculture to increase the productivity per hectare. Labour power shortages in agriculture have to be overcome. When machine operators cannot work on their machines they must go to the fields. Office workers in agricultural enterprises must be reduced by some 80 per cent. If Cuba is to have the food it requires, agricultural workers have to be paid adequate wages, even higher than in the city and new homes must be built where needed, as well as day-care centres for agricultural workers' children.

The second programme to be maintained is biotechnology, the pharmaceutical industry and research centres because they offer a 'world of resources' to the country. Castro believes that the industry is capable of producing any medication that the imperialists are capable of producing and others that they are not producing. The third programme to be maintained will be the tourist industry which can bring in large revenues for Cuba. These are the top priority programmes. Any economic programme which gives the country something, saves imports, solves an important problem or generates exports will have priority attention. These will be given priority over various social programmes and projects such as building new schools to replace old ones in the capital, although everything that has been started will, if possible, be completed.

Saving fuel will be a priority. Petrol rationing has been introduced and household electricity supplies cut. In agriculture oxen will be trained to replace machinery. 200,000 bicycles have already been bought and arrangements have been made to buy 500,000 more as well as buying machinery to set up five bicycle factories. Sales of electrical appliances will be reduced and no more air conditioners will be sold. If, because of shortages of materials etc, the hours worked need to be reduced then the emphasis will be on reducing the number of days worked rather than hours per working day in order to cut down the number of journeys necessary in travelling to work and so save fuel.

Only a socialist system can confront these problems

How would the capitalists deal with the kind of problems Cuba faces? They would double or triple the prices of electricity or transportation to deal with a shortfall of fuel. Production would be cut and transportation withdrawn with the inevitable massive loss of jobs. 'Who would be hurt the most, who would it affect? The workers, the poorest sector of the population.'

In many Latin American countries, even before the full effects of the oil crisis, thousands of people are being thrown out on the street, prices are multiplying, the people are harassed and only a minority of the very privileged can solve their problems. The World Bank and IMF 'shock' programmes recommended to many of the formerly socialist countries in Eastern Europe, those which have decided to become capitalist, mean millions of people being kicked out on the street and prices going up.

The Cuban strategy for dealing with the economic crisis rules out mass lay-offs and price increases.

'The Revolution will confront the problems during this special period without throwing anyone out of work and without depriving a single citizen of her or his resources . . . No, we will not abandon a single person – this is a characteristic of our socialism, our system . . . We are looking at many formulas but none at the expense of the citizenry. At worst, the worker will get more free time but he will never be left out in the street without a job or penniless. That's a truly humane concept.

The imperialists talk so much about human rights and their formulas are so ruthless, always at the expense of the workers, always at the expense of the people. That will be the great virtue of our system in dealing with difficulties such as these.'

The crisis in the socialist camp and the energy crisis stemming from the

Gulf has created extremely serious problems for the Cuban Revolution. Inevitably there will be those who lose their morale and try to spread demoralisation. They have to be confronted. In difficult times the *gusanos* (counter-revolutionaries) raise their heads attacking socialism and calling for the restoration of capitalism. They must be told 'Gusano back to your hole'. In defending socialist Cuba, Castro says that the people are being asked to carry out an extraordinary internationalist mission.

'Saving the Revolution in Cuba and saving socialism in Cuba ... will be the greatest internationalist service that our people can render humanity.'

Castro is confident that difficult times and setbacks faced by revolutionaries are temporary ones. 'Revolutionary ideas haven't become obsolete ... they're going through difficult times but they'll return with added strength.' They will return all the sooner the more injustice, the more exploitation, the more hunger and greater chaos in the world. For the present, however, it falls on the Cuban people to be the standard bearers of revolutionary ideas, 'to raise them up high, for that's the mission history has assigned to us'. ■

All quotes are from a speech on 28 September 1990, published in *Granma* 14 October 1990

4.3 IN DEFENCE OF SOCIALISM
DAVID REED
FRFI 103 · OCTOBER/NOVEMBER 1991

The collapse of the socialist bloc and the counter-revolution in the Soviet Union have inevitably focussed attention on the future of socialism in Cuba. Capitalist propaganda portrays Fidel Castro as an isolated and lonely figure and the Cuban Revolution as facing its last days. But those rushing to write the epitaph for the communist ideal underestimate Fidel Castro and the Cuban people. 'To those who think that there could be no future for [Cuba], we have to answer that the only thing that could never have a future would be a country without independence, without revolution and without socialism' (*Granma* Editorial 8 September 1991).

That Fidel Castro was able to attend and address the First Ibero-American Summit in Guadalajara, Mexico, in July, against the expressed wishes of the United States; that positions advanced by Cuba, on the democratisation of the United Nations and the right of every nation to choose its political system and institutions, were in the final document of the Summit; and that Chile and Colombia took advantage of the Summit to establish diplomatic ties with Cuba shows, far from being isolated, the enhanced standing Cuba has among the Latin American countries.

In two recent speeches*, including that to the Ibero-American Summit, given before the counter-revolution in the Soviet Union, Fidel Castro confronts the triumphalism of US imperialism and the headlong retreat of a great proportion of the world's left forces with a sustained and eloquent defence of socialism. He argues that the problems of economic development, poverty and inequality cannot be resolved by capitalism in a world which is divided between immensely rich capitalist countries and the majority of extremely poor countries, precisely as a consequence of capitalism, colonialism, neocolonialism and imperialism. 'In this world to think that neo-liberal formulas are going to promote the miracle of economic development ... is an incredible delusion' (B p12).

A new world order worse than the old?

A substantial restructuring of international relations is taking place as a result of the collapse of socialism in the Soviet Union and Eastern Europe. The conflict between two antagonistic blocs is no longer the focus of those relations. While this has significantly reduced the danger of nuclear holocaust and confrontation between the two major military powers, the new world order could well be worse than the old, especially for the peoples of the Third World.

* A Speech to the First Ibero-American Summit, *Granma* 4 August 1991
  B Speech on 26 July 1991, *Granma* 11 August 1991.

While a new type of relationship is being established between the superpowers, acts of brutal intervention can take place in the Third World as the invasion of Panama and the Gulf war demonstrated. 'An unscrupulous hegemonic perspective and practice prevails' in US ruling circles, 'which see themselves as the victors of the so-called cold war'. The greatest threat to the principles of international law and, above all, to a permanent halt to interference in the internal affairs of other countries is the political and military hegemony of the United States. With the so-called 'Soviet threat' gone, the US ruling class, under the guise of strengthening US national security, believes it can face the challenge of regional conflicts, low-intensity wars, the drug trade and subversion, by any means it sees fit and according to its own interpretation in each case. 'The most likely scenarios for all the above – but not the only ones – are in the Third World.'

'In the end the new world order could be worse than the old order, a unipolar world in which the cessation of antagonism between blocs, exalted by some as the end of ideology and the triumph of universal values, is due above all to the extinction of the socialist community, while the imperialist system of economic and political relations continues, now without rival, subjugating and maintaining the principal contradiction with the Third World.' A p5

The economic decline of US imperialism

While the United States is more powerful than ever in military terms and politically has enormous influence, economically it is weaker than ever and is facing serious problems. Castro tells us that when a US journalist interviewing him said that the USSR had been ruined by the arms race with the United States he replied: 'The USSR might be the first to be ruined, but you will be the second . . . Don't sing victory songs' (B p13).

After World War II, the United States was the centre of capitalism, the richest and most competitive of all countries. It enjoyed complete hegemony, but now it has lost this position. The powers defeated in

World War II have emerged as poles for the concentration of economic power, defying US supremacy (A p5). The US cannot compete with Europe, dominated by Germany, nor with Japan.

The following economic statistics illustrate the economic problems facing the United States. In the years after the war the rate of return on US capital was as high as 24 per cent. Now it is about a third of that rate, around 8 per cent.

Historically the United States has had a high savings rate. Today it has fallen to about five cents out of every dollar earned. This is to be compared with savings as high as 30 cents in some European countries.

The total debt in the United States – federal and private – is $10 trillion. The federal government accounts for about three trillion and the rest is owed by businesses and individuals. The country has a debt double the size of its GNP. As a result of the recession that began in the middle of 1990, it has been announced that the budget deficit for the fiscal year which begins in October 1991 will be $350 billion – an amazing statistic even for as large an economy as the United States.

The United States not only has a trade deficit of $100 billion but now has an overall foreign debt of more than $600 billion. Only ten years ago it had a credit of some $140 billion with the rest of the world. In having such a large budget and trade deficit, the United States does exactly what it prohibits other countries from doing.

The economic indebtedness of the United States will have enormous consequences for the rest of the world especially the former socialist countries and the Third World desperate for capital to develop their economies. 'According to experts, the demand for money in the world is over $200 billion more than what is available.' There is not enough capital to satisfy the demands of Latin America, the Middle East, the Eastern European countries and the

CUBANS DEFEND SOCIALISM

121

Soviet Union. 'The United States has become an octopus, sucking up huge quantities of money, and they themselves need more than anyone else' (B p13).

The United States foreign trade and debt position is of a country losing ground to its competitors in Europe and Japan. To reverse this position it will be necessary to reinforce its area of influence, its economic space, and to reaffirm its dominion (A p3). This is the context in which its recent initiatives for the Americas should be seen, in particular the proposal to create a free trade zone. Castro, in his speech to the First Ibero-American Summit, said that if Latin America is going to integrate into the economy of a financially ruined country it is going to get the worst end of the deal.

Sixty per cent of Latin American exports to the United States are fuel and raw materials, while less than 30 per cent are manufactured products. The situation has deteriorated over the last 20 years. In 1970 38.2 per cent came into the category of manufactured products, compared with 29 per cent in 1988. The main cause of this drop was US protectionist policy, which tended to block the most finished products and favour raw materials. This protectionist policy, based on non-tariff barriers, would not be affected by this 'free trade' initiative, which is nothing more than an attempt to control Latin America's trade, using the US's technical and scientific superiority and competitive capacity. It will reinforce the neo-colonial structure of the region's foreign trade (A p4).

Compared to its trade with the United States, trade among Latin American countries is insignificant accounting for only 13.9 per cent of total Latin American exports. During his speech Castro argued that Latin America had no alternative but to integrate economically if it was to develop in the face of the increasingly powerful and protectionist economic powers: the United States, the European Community and Japan. And that Cuba could be part of this process without renouncing socialism (A pp4, 6; B p13).

Capitalism and Latin America

1991 is the tenth consecutive year of Latin America's worst economic crisis in the current century. 1990 per capita GNP was equal to that of 1977. Latin America's foreign debt is unpayable – a point made by Fidel Castro in 1985. Latin America which owed $222.5 billion in 1980, paid out in principal and interest $365.9 billion in the last decade. But by 1990 the debt was $423 billion. So the debt nearly doubled in spite of the enormous amount paid back. Inflation, which averaged 56.1 per cent in 1982, in 1990, after several years of neoliberal policies, reached the nearly incredible average of 1,500 per cent.

There are 270 million poor people in Latin America, 62 per cent of the population, of which 84 million are destitute. This poverty of the majority drastically contrasts with the opulence of small minorities. In some cases five per cent of the population receives up to 50 per cent of the income while 30 or 40 per cent of the population receives ten per cent.

Between 20 and 30 million homeless children roam the streets of Latin America. Thirty to 40 per cent of the workforce is unemployed or underemployed; malnutrition affects 80 to 100 million people. Life expectancy is 68 years, seven years less than in the developed countries. The infant mortality rate is 55 per 1,000 live births. Twenty-one per cent of the population have no access to safe drinking water, and 41 per cent lack adequate health facilities. Only 44 children out of 100 who enrol for elementary school across Latin America finish it. The critical situation of housing and its rapid deterioration over the past few years has led to the proliferation of shanty towns and slums throughout the continent. With the rapid growth of the urban population housing covered only 24 per cent of the needs between 1985 and 1989. It has been estimated that some $282 billion would be needed to bring health, housing and education to adequate standards in Latin America (A p2, 3).

All this poverty from which the Latin American countries suffer is the direct result of capitalism. Yet we are confronted with more and more theories on how private enterprise creates wealth and social justice requires capitalism, private enterprise and the market economy. The

123

reality is quite different as a comparison with socialist Cuba so clearly demonstrates.

Socialism and Cuba

Throughout its existence socialist Cuba has had not only to confront the many obstacles facing any development process in a Third World country but has also had to face a rigid economic blockade of the country imposed by the United States since 1961 – depriving the country, on the basis of the most conservative calculations, of $15 billion of resources over the last 30 years. The construction of a more just and humane society in these circumstances is an historic feat of the Cuban people and Cuban socialism.

The catastrophic social conditions which exist throughout Latin America do not exist in Cuba. The infant mortality rate in Cuba at 10.7 per 1,000 live births is better than in many developed countries. Life expectancy is 76 years of age and rising. Illiteracy disappeared some time ago. Nearly 100 per cent of the children who enter elementary school finish and more than 90 per cent of those of the appropriate age are in secondary school. There are no shanty towns. Malnutrition is almost unknown in Cuba. Unemployment is practically non-existent. The whole population is protected by social security, has the right to education and to free health care, even if they need a heart transplant. There are no beggars in the street nor abandoned elderly people; and the generalised climate of violence which characterises the great majority of contemporary societies is not found in Cuba. That is Cuban socialism (A pp4, 5; B p13).

Since the second half of 1989, Cuba has had to deal with the collapse of the socialist countries. Three quarters of Cuba's trade had been with those countries on just and reasonable terms. As a result, Cuba has been forced to introduce an emergency programme to survive, a special period, starting in the last quarter of 1990. Living standards have fallen and increasingly severe rationing of basic goods is becoming necessary. Cuba now faces very serious economic problems. The measures it is taking to cope, however, have nothing in common with the well-known adjustment policies of the International Monetary Fund. They have been adopted according to the principle of adequate protection for all citizens. No one will be put out on the street, no one will be unemployed. 'We distribute what we have and that is socialism, that is social justice . . . if we have a lot we can distribute a lot and if we have little, we distribute a little, but we'll distribute what we have, we won't abandon anyone' (B p13).

Throughout its existence socialist Cuba has demonstrated in practice the meaning of socialist internationalism. Cuban socialists have given their lives for the struggle for freedom and democracy in other parts of the world, especially in Latin America and Africa. Today with US imperialism accelerating efforts to strangle Cuba, internationalism must focus on defending the Cuban Revolution – it is the greatest service that not only Cuban socialists but socialists everywhere can offer humanity.

■

4.4 US IMPERIALISM TIGHTENS THE BLOCKADE
CAT WIENER
FRFI 107 · JUNE/JULY 1992

On 18 April the Bush Administration responded to the surge of international solidarity with Cuba by endorsing an intensification of the US blockade of Cuba, in defiance of international law. The draft legislation, proposed by Democrat Senator Robert Torricelli, will prohibit the access to US ports of any boat trading with Cuba without special permission. This violates internationally recognised laws of the sea which prevent any state from imposing pressure, coercion or any other limits on the open maritime trade and the freedom of navigation.

Around the world, solidarity campaigns are sending ships filled with medicines, powdered milk, oil, grain and other necessities to Cuba to break the embargo. This action reflects a degree of political support which is urgently needed: however, it is clear that mobilisation on a far wider scale is still essential if the embattled Cuban economy is to survive.

Support is coming from China, from Australia, from Spain – but particularly from Latin America. On the day Bush announced the tightening of the blockade, 222 representatives from 27 countries in Latin America and the Caribbean met at the Cuban Institute of Friendship with the Peoples (ICAP) to re-pledge their solidarity with the Cuban Revolution and draw up a plan of action which includes an international campaign to send fuel and school materials to Cuba; to collect signatures opposing the US blockade and calling for recognition of Cuba's sovereignty and an end to hostile political and military action. As poverty, disease and misery intensify in the rest of Latin America, socialist Cuba has the potential to become the lynch-pin of struggle against US imperialism. In the words of the Dominican delegate, 'to defend Cuba is to defend Latin America and the Caribbean.'

This unity creates something of a dilemma for the Bush administration. With an election in the offing, and facing a challenge from the right, Bush is anxious not to be seen as 'soft on Cuba'. At the same time, he does not want to provide the impetus that would push Latin American countries, already sympathetic to Cuba, into open hostility. For this reason, he opposed the section of the Toricelli Bill that proposed cutting off aid to Latin American countries who trade with Cuba.

More insidious is the propaganda war being waged by imperialism to create a political climate which permits the stepping up of the US's economic stranglehold on Cuba, while keeping alive the possibility of a Panama-style military attack. To this end, the media lackeys of papers such as the British *Guardian* and *Independent* trot out once again the hackneyed lies: 'Cuba stays out of US war on cocaine trade', with articles implying that Cuba is a safe haven for drug traffickers. No matter to these hacks that Cuba's offer to the US to collaborate on drugs information was time after time ignored – so that even a Republican senator was driven to cry out in frustration 'For God's sake, it is drugs not communists that are killing our children!' No matter that the US administration is itself deeply implicated in the laundering of drugs money from Latin America; that when General Ochoa was convicted of involvement in drug running he was shot (but then, of course, our hypocrites change their tune to one of 'human rights'). They choose not to write about the Cuban ship illegally stopped and searched by

Mexican coast-guards who found – nothing. Most of the 'evidence' relied on comes from the group of viciously reactionary Cuban exiles living in Miami, professional counter-revolutionaries who have sold their souls for dollars – so that even Washington Cuba policy experts are forced to concede 'Washington is highly suspicious of reports coming out of Miami'. Yet the rumours are fomented, providing the excuse for incursions into Cuban airspace and waters, and 'intelligence gathering'.

Meanwhile, in Cuba, as the first fruits of the agricultural programme began to appear on the shelves, potatoes, tomatoes, bananas, gradually being supplemented by material aid from Mexico, Australia and Europe, the Cuban people took to the streets in their tens of thousands to celebrate May Day and loudly proclaim their defiance of US imperialism and their support for Cuba, for the Revolution, and for socialism. ■

PART FIVE

Uphold the banner of communism!

5.1 THE TRIUMPH OF IMPERIALISM?
DAVID REED
FRFI 96 · AUGUST/SEPTEMBER 1990

The leaders of the major imperialist nations were in triumphal mood as they emerged from the NATO summit in London and the Group of Seven (G7) economic summit in Houston in 1990. A 'turning point in history' (Bush after NATO summit); the 'renaissance of democracy' (final communiqué, Houston meeting) were claimed as imperialism celebrated what it regarded as a total economic and political victory over communism. Freedom and prosperity were indissolubly linked with private enterprise and capitalism, communism with economic failure and dictatorship.

In Eastern Europe imperialism has forced open areas of the world previously closed to its economic exploitation for more than four decades. The Soviet Union is in retreat, the Communist Party in disarray, rapidly breaking away from the legacy and traditions rising from the Bolshevik Revolution. Under Gorbachev, class struggle has been abandoned in favour of 'universal human values'. Internationally, the previous commitment to the Third World is gradually being replaced by a more opportunistic and conciliatory approach to imperialism. Economically the Soviet Union's future is more and more dependent on loans and investment from imperialism. Fred Halliday has accurately summed up the situation: 'After decades of partial success, (the socialist countries) now appear to have succumbed to a mode of production and a political system far stronger than them, and which does not appear to be headed for any predetermined exhaustion or crisis.' (*New Left Review* 180).

Is then the triumphal mood of the major imperialist powers justified? With the demise of the socialist bloc can the imperialist powers maintain harmonious and cooperative relations between themselves to ensure continuing economic stability or will the inter-imperialist rivalries of earlier periods re-emerge?

The London and Houston summits, in spite of all the triumphalism, could not conceal major differences between the imperialist powers. At the Houston summit there were three main areas of disagreement: farm subsidies, the environment, and aid to the Soviet Union. The compromise on farm subsidies did little more than delay the inevitable confrontation at the Gatt trade liberalisation talks beginning on 23 July.

An ever present factor at both meetings was the re-emergence of a united Germany as the overwhelmingly dominant economic and political power at the centre of the European imperialist bloc. In the past NATO linked the United States and Europe in an anti-communist political and military bloc controlled by US imperialism. Today it has to serve other needs as well. Only a strong NATO, retaining US troops in Europe as well as nuclear weapons, could possibly harness and control the imperialist ambitions of a united Germany.

Gorbachev was offered a face saving formula – an empty gesture – to get the Soviet Union to accept German reunification within NATO. Nuclear weapons were now 'weapons of last resort', there would be a strengthened pan-European Conference on Security and Co-operation, and he and a few others would be invited to NATO headquarters in Brussels. This changed nothing. The 'first use' doctrine would remain now as before, under which NATO reserves the right to use nuclear weapons when conventional forces are unable to resist attack. Thatcher, increasingly frustrated with Britain being relegated by Germany to a secondary role in world economic and political affairs, was particularly insistent on this point. She had inserted in the final declaration the sentence: 'there are no circumstances in which nuclear retaliation in response to military action might be discounted.'

Britain has been the imperialist power most undermined by the rise of German imperialism. The special relationship with US imperialism is no longer sustainable. Thatcher, having tried to prevent the reunification of Germany, is fighting a rearguard action to stop Britain becoming a secondary imperialist power in a European bloc dominated by German imperialism. The British ruling class has split on this issue. Nicholas Ridley's anti-German outburst on European monetary policy only gave vent to the frustrated imperialist ambitions of a section of the ruling class. 'This is a German racket designed to take over the whole of Europe. It has to be thwarted . . . '. Handing sovereignty to the European Community, he said, was like handling it over to Hitler.

At the Houston summit the imperialist powers were divided on the question of economic loans and aid to the Soviet Union. The USA, Britain and Japan, recognising Germany's superior position to exploit the opportunities opened up by the destruction of the socialist bloc, were hoping to delay the process giving themselves more time to improve their position. All argued for aid conditional on, essentially, the progress made in restoring capitalism in the Soviet Union and the withdrawal of its support for socialist and other progressive regimes – 'to cut support from nations promoting regional conflict'. Of primary concern is their determination to destroy the Cuban Revolution. The US wants outstanding debts to be paid – in particular the $300 million borrowed by the Tsarist and Kerensky governments before the Revolution and $700 million from lend–lease during the Second World War before it will give any financial assistance. The Japanese want the Soviet Union to surrender the four Kurile islands it has held since the end of the war. No agreement could be made.

German and French imperialism will proceed with their own $15 billion package for the Soviet Union. Just as Japan will offer a $5 billion credit to China. Each imperialist power will manoeuvre to gain the stronger position. 'Principles' will be pushed aside for profit-making. With the end of US domination, and the emergence of three more equally matched imperialist blocs: the US, Japan and Germany, new conflicts are inevitable. The Houston summit, in the words of the *Financial Times*, only 'papered over the cracks'.

5.2 COMMUNISM AND SOCIAL DEMOCRACY – THE GREAT DIVIDE
DAVID REED & EDDIE ABRAHAMS
FRFI 93 · FEBRUARY/MARCH 1990

Fight Racism! Fight Imperialism!'s assessment of the crisis afflicting the Soviet Union and Eastern Europe fundamentally diverges from that of the rest of the British left. Whereas we recognise the counter-revolutionary essence of the political processes taking place, the rest of the left hails them as popular revolutions against totalitarian regimes.

Whilst we have seen in these developments the first stages in the restoration of capitalism, the British left has variously welcomed them as a defeat for Stalinism not for socialism (orthodox Trotskyists), the end of the Leninist, and in some cases, the Marxist legacy (various factions of the CPGB) and even the revolutionary assertion of workers' power (SWP).

What is the basis for our sharp and irreconcilable opposition to the British left on this question? Political developments are assessed from a class standpoint. We are communists. 'In the national struggles of the proletarians of different countries communists point out and bring to the front the common interests of the entire proletariat independent of all nationality.' (*Communist Manifesto*). Today the common interests of the proletariat are, and can only be, expressed through the struggle to destroy imperialism: that is the worldwide capitalist system which denies the vast majority of humanity the prospect of ever escaping poverty, hunger, disease and oppression. Whether a political movement is progressive or reactionary depends, therefore, on whether it advances or retards the struggle to destroy imperialism.

How then should political developments in Eastern Europe be judged on these criteria? Imperialism is jubilant. A whole area of the world once closed to the unrestrained marauding of its multinationals and banks, is

131

now available for limitless exploitation and profit making. The real essence of this development has been sharply outlined by Fidel Castro:

> 'Imperialism is urging the European socialist countries to become recipients of its surplus capital, to develop capitalism and to join in plundering the Third World countries . . . an invitation which seems not to displease the theoreticians of capitalist reform. Thus in many of those (socialist) countries no one speaks about the tragedy of the Third World, and their discontented multitudes are guided towards capitalism and anti-communism – and, in one country, towards Pan-Germanism. Such developments may even lead to fascist trends. The prize promised by imperialism is a share of the plunder rested from our peoples, the only way of building capitalist consumer societies.'

It is through this plunder of the Third World that imperialism has been able to sustain capitalist consumer societies as a mechanism to secure the loyalty of substantial layers of the working class in the imperialist countries. The political expression of this subordination of the working class to imperialism is social democracy.

It is the promise of such consumer societies that has proved so attractive to the privileged layers of the working class and professional strata in the socialist bloc. That is why social democracy, aided, advised and financed by its political counterparts in Western Europe, is rapidly becoming the dominant trend within the organised political movement in Eastern Europe. It was to consolidate this alliance that in the first week of February, Neil Kinnock joined 19 other West European social democratic leaders in the People's Theatre on East Berlin's Luxemburg Strasse to answer questions and debate with an East German audience. So who has gained from developments in Eastern Europe, who are the beneficiaries? Certainly not the socialist countries of the Third World, the liberation movements fighting imperialism, the working class of Eastern Europe or the oppressed and exploited millions throughout Africa, Asia, Latin America and the Middle East. It is imperialism that is expecting a new lease of life from the counter-revolution and in its wake will crawl social democracy, its longstanding and trusted servant in the working class movement.

To understand why the British left has taken a fundamentally social democratic position on Eastern Europe we must examine its class roots. The relative prosperity in the imperialist nations during the post-war boom gave rise to a new, relatively privileged section of the working class – a new petit bourgeoisie. This layer of predominantly educated, salaried white-collar workers grew with the expansion of the state and services sector and, in the more recent period, with the information technology 'revolution'. This layer has always had privileged access to a 'capitalist consumer society'.

The British left draws its membership primarily from this layer and adapts to all its political prejudices, narrowness and Eurocentricity. This is the foundation of its apparently unbreakable bond with social democracy and its refusal to risk this privilege by politically confronting British imperialism.

Marxism Today has given the most articulate exposition of the left social democratic standpoint on the lessons of Eastern Europe. Crucial to its position is the view that the historic split in the international labour movement between social democracy and communism has no further justification. This standpoint is based on two reactionary assumptions. One, that the collapse of socialism in Eastern Europe shows that Leninism is dead, as is the Bolshevik form of revolutionary struggle.

'Stalinism is dead, and Leninism – its theory of the state, its concept of the party, the absence of civil society, its notion of revolution – has also had its day.'
MARTIN JACQUES, MARXISM TODAY, JANUARY 1990

Second, they argue that since the 1950s it has been quite clear that the capitalist system 'is more than viable'. Eric Hobsbawm argues that unlike the period between 1914 and the early 1950s when world capitalism was in a period of catastrophic crisis, today: 'In so far as we envisage a change in the nature of capitalism, it will not, within the forseeable future, be through a basic catastrophic crisis of the capitalist system, out of which the only thing that can be saved is by revolutionary means.' (ibid)

Some, such as Gareth Steadman Jones, have already drawn the logic of these two assumptions by stating that Marxism itself is 'a set of unsubstantiated claims.' (*Marxism Today* February 1990).

The social and material basis for these views has been brilliantly parodied by A Sivanandan when he defined their socialism as an 'eat, drink and be merry socialism because tomorrow we can eat, drink and be merry again, a socialism for disillusioned Marxist intellectuals who had waited around too long for the revolution . . . ' (*Race and Class*). It is the class standpoint of the privileged new petit bourgeoisie who have more than adequate access to the 'capitalist consumer society'.

But what of the one third of British society (or indeed any advanced capitalist society today), that substantial minority which find itself shut out from the benefits of prosperity? *Marxism Today* calls for a European-wide Keynesianism. Arguing correctly that the old vision of 1945, of a Keynesian welfare society is no longer sustainable on a national basis, their solution is a pan-European one. In the words of Achille Occhetto, the leader of the Italian Communist Party:

> 'Yes national Keynesianism has come to an end, which means the end of those policies of redistribution on a national level in which the labour movement took part, and which at the same time also helped to reinforce it. The national dimension has failed and we must find an overall European alternative.'
>
> MARXISM TODAY, FEBRUARY 1990

The collapse of the socialist bloc and the re-emergence of social democracy in Eastern Europe has created precisely the opening for a pan-European supranational Keynesian project. Such a project depends on the consolidation of the alliance between European social democracy and a strong European imperialism at the expense of the majority of the working class in Eastern Europe and the Soviet Union, and the oppressed peoples of the Third World. This is why *Marxism Today* cannot approach the developments in Eastern Europe as communists must – and ask whether they advance or retard the struggle to destroy imperialism.

Unlike *Marxism Today*, the Trotskyist left attempts to impose a revolutionary, and not social democratic, gloss on the disintegration of the socialist bloc. In reality by applauding this disintegration they end up necessarily in the camp of social democracy and counter-revolution. This happens because their idealism, their Trotskyist theology, does not deign to recognise the very real existence of imperialism. The notion that the destruction of the Eastern European regimes by mass protest movements will leave intact the socialist foundation of these states is naive idealism. Imperialism and its social democratic allies are well organised and have limitless resources at their disposal to ensure that these socialist foundations are destroyed. The communist movement, non-existent in the imperialist countries, too weak elsewere, is at the moment incapable of preventing this development.

British Trotskyism has, as a result of its petit bourgeois idealism, supported and indeed openly financed counter-revolutionary forces in Eastern Europe. In the early 1980s they were unanimous in supporting Solidarity in Poland and its leader Lech Walesa. Today those forces are implementing a vicious attack on the working class at the behest of imperialism, and Walesa has been touting around Poland's assets to the imperialists. We remind the SWP, who regard all socialist countries as state-capitalist regimes, that in the late 1960s they were peddling the views of Jacek Kuron, as those of a 'brilliant Marxist' calling for a return to 'real socialism based on workers' councils and workers' control of production'. Today Jacek Kuron, as Minister of Labour in Poland, is directing the IMF's vicious austerity programme against the Polish working class. Anti-communists in reality have strange bedfellows.

As a result of developments in the socialist bloc, the communist and anti-imperialist movement has been severely weakened. Imperialism has

BERLIN WALL, 1989

135

been immeasurably strengthened. With the inevitable strengthening of social democracy, communists in Britain will for a whole period suffer severe isolation. The revolutionary struggle against imperialism will intensify as imperialism intensifies its plunder of the oppressed nations. There will be more revolutions and more rebellions in these nations. British communists, carrying on the traditions of Marx, Engels and Lenin to liberate humanity from the chains of capitalism must continue the hard and difficult work of winning the British working class to the side of those fighting imperialism. ■

5.3 UPHOLD THE BANNER OF COMMUNISM
DAVID REED/EDDIE ABRAHAMS
FRFI 103 · OCTOBER/NOVEMBER 1991

The August 1991 counter-revolution in the USSR was a massive blow to the international working class and to the vast majority of humanity. Only hardened anti-Soviet dogmatists and middle-class intellectuals of the imperialist countries, living in affluent conditions afforded them by imperialist plunder of the Third World, could argue otherwise. The collapse of the socialist bloc, for the time being, leaves the imperialist economic and political system without rival, all the more able to subjugate challenges to its aggressive and expansionist drives.

Far from moderating imperialism's predatory character, the collapse of the socialist bloc has removed all constraints on its drive to carve up and divide the world. The danger of war now looms larger as three powerful capitalist economic blocs – USA, Japan and German-led Europe – compete for the spoils of the Soviet Union and Eastern Europe. As the crisis of the capitalist world intensifies these major world powers will seek once again to divide and redivide the world according to the balance of economic power. Unless imperialism is destroyed humanity will be threatened with a new imperialist war.

The counter-revolution is a calamity for the Soviet people. Its consequences are terrifying, and promise in the words of Russian socialist Boris Kagarlitsky, 'a new Brazil just waiting to be Latin Americanised'.

Whilst a small minority will prosper, millions will be driven into destitution. Malnutrition, unemployment, homelessness and social deprivation will become rampant as the gains of the October Revolution are rapidly dismantled. The disintegration of the Soviet Union heralds a return to vicious and bloody national conflict and a resurgence of Great Russian chauvinism, reactionary nationalism, racism and anti-Semitism. Only hardened reactionaries could welcome this counter-revolution.

Internationally the collapse of the Soviet Union leaves all socialist, progressive and anti-imperialist movements vulnerable. Despite its problems, the Soviet Union was a force for democracy and freedom. It defeated fascism and Hitler. Without it the revolutions in China, Korea, Vietnam and Cuba would not have survived for so long. Without it the liberation struggles in Africa, Asia, the Middle East and Latin America would have paid an immeasurably higher price. As Alexander Cockburn, an honest voice opposing ingrained Western mendacity, so rightly remarks:

'Without the Soviet Union, just such a relatively independent country as India could have taken instead, the course of fascist Argentina ... It was communists who spearheaded the fight for civil rights in the United States in the 1930s, and without the threat of the Soviet model for the Third World, the US probably would not even have bothered to desegregate the army after the war ... There would never have been International Brigades ... to defend the young [Spanish] republic against Franco, fascism and the complicity of the Western powers.'
NEW STATESMAN 30 AUGUST 1991

As Cockburn says, you can write your own list.

The collapse of Soviet socialism

The imperialists and their social democratic allies are celebrating what they regard as the demise of communism. Their celebrations are premature. Unlike capitalism whose foundations go back many centuries, socialism is in its infancy. Marx and Engels initially envisaged socialism being built on the basis of the most advanced economic achievements of capitalism. Historical developments, and in particular the transformation of capitalism into imperialism, dictated otherwise.

The world's first socialist state was established a mere 74 years ago and in a backward semi-feudal country with a tiny working class. From its inception it was encircled by economically more powerful enemies and received little of the expected support from the mass working class movements in the imperialist countries. Lenin's hopes of building and consolidating Russian socialism in alliance with victorious revolutions in Western Europe floundered on the national chauvinism and backwardness of the organised working class movements in the more developed capitalist countries. As Rosa Luxemburg succinctly argued:

> 'All of us are subject to the laws of history, and it is only internationally that the socialist order of society can be realised. The Bolsheviks have shown that they are capable of everything that a genuine revolutionary party can contribute within the limits of historical possibilities. They are not supposed to perform miracles. For a model and faultless proletarian revolution in an isolated land, exhausted by world war, strangled by imperialism, betrayed by the international proletariat, would be a miracle.'
> THE RUSSIAN REVOLUTION, 1918

In these circumstances, the Bolsheviks had no choice. Against enormous odds they had to hold on to political power and take the first tentative steps to build socialism. The alternative was handing over Russian workers and the oppressed peasantry to the merciless revenge of a bloody counter-revolution. Yet today such a surrender would have been, it seems, the preferred option of middle class socialist intellectuals who have rediscovered the renegade Kautsky.

During the struggle for survival, the Revolution was forced to retreat. It was to face foreign military intervention, civil war, world war and relentless imperialist economic and political aggression. Inevitably, this took its toll on the Communist Party of Soviet Union. As the revolutionary impetus dwindled the Party lost its connection with the masses, time serving careerists replaced revolutionaries and privilege replaced sacrifice and eventually communism lapsed into social democracy.

In these conditions the Communist Party could not tackle, let alone solve, the critical questions of the relationship between the Party, the working class and democracy; between the centralised economic plan, the market and socialist democracy; and between the defence of Soviet power and proletarian internationalism. But new revolutionaries, following the path that the Bolsheviks dared to tread, are learning and will continue to learn from the lessons of this historical experience, enriching it through their own struggle to build socialism. Real revolutionaries follow the traditions of Marx and Engels. After the bloody defeat of the Paris Commune they did not condemn them for daring to seize power. Rather they drew the lessons of that experience for future generations who would follow the same courageous path in attempting to build a just and humane society.

One critical lesson to be learnt is argued in Che Guevara's study of the Soviet economic planning. Che rejected the view that economic planning could be separated from the production and reproduction of communist social relations and consciousness. The planned economy and socialism would develop successfully only if they ran parallel with the development of a new communist social consciousness. The latter does not arise automatically, it flows from the ideological and political work of a communist leadership.

Such a leadership had long ceased to exist in the Soviet Union. The consequence was an attempt to solve the crisis of the Soviet economy by capitalist methods. Hence *perestroika* – the resort to so-called 'market socialism', the law of value, competition, market forces, material incentives and private enterprise. These created the conditions for producing and reproducing capitalist social relations in the Soviet Union.

GULF WAR – RCG ON THE MARCH

The resistance to this by the working class and sections of the *nomenklatura* led to a paralysis and subsequent catastrophic collapse of the Soviet economy. Pro-capitalist forces supported by sections of the Party and the privileged stratum of professionals, managers and intellectuals now recognised that the old state had to be destroyed as a condition for the restoration of capitalism in the Soviet Union. The coup created the opportunity for this to be done. Yeltsin and his followers seized the opportunity presented by the staggering incompetence of the 19 August coup leaders to take state power – the counter-revolution was underway. He was assured of the backing of the main imperialist powers.

The British left and the counter-revolution

With few exceptions (eg, *The Leninist*), the British left joined in the imperialist celebrations of the counter-revolution. How could *Militant* tell us that 'workers around the world are cheering'? How could *Socialist Worker* not only support the Yeltsin counter-revolution but, staggeringly, celebrate 'the destruction of the statues of Marx and Lenin – those symbols of oppression for millions of workers'? (*Socialist Worker* 7 September 1991). How is it that the once staunchly pro-Soviet CPGB praises Yeltsin's 'courage' in carrying out the counter-revolution? To understand this we have to understand the relationship that these organisations have to social democracy and imperialism.

Social democracy is the product of imperialism. Its social base is the privileged layers of the working class. These privileges arise from the sustained prosperity of the major capitalist nations, a prosperity dependent on the super-exploitation of oppressed nations. Social democracy's opposition to the Soviet Union rested on the Soviet Union's fundamental break with imperialism. By removing whole areas of the world from the sphere of imperialist exploitation and profit-making the mere existence of the USSR made it an intractable enemy of social democracy.

The post-war boom created a new privileged strata of predominantly educated and salaried white-collar workers in the imperialist nations.

140

Their privileges rested on the continuation of imperialism. The British left draws its membership primarily from this strata. This explains its unbreakable bond with social democracy and its consistent refusal to oppose imperialism. This is why the Trotskyists and the 'Stalinists' can end up on the same side supporting Yeltsin's counter-revolution. The Trotskyists' hatred for the Communist Party of the Soviet Union and their opportunist ties to social democracy, blinded them to the USSR's essentially anti-imperialist character. It forced them, at all critical turning points, into the imperialist camp.

The 'Stalinists'' pro-Sovietism, on the other hand, was always of a formal character retaining as it did unbreakable ties to social democracy since the 1930s. Indeed, recent evidence shows that even Stalin criticised the CPGB for its unprincipled support for the Labour Party in its draft programme *The British Road To Socialism*. Its opportunism, as always, arose not through its relationship to the Soviet Communist Party, but from its close bonds with social democracy. Parallel with its abandonment of any links with the communist tradition, the CPGB abandonned even a formal pro-Soviet stand and degenerated into a support group for Kinnock's Labour Party.

British Trotskyism and 'Stalinism' are mirror images – anti-Soviet and pro-Soviet left wing covers for social democracy. The collapse of the CPSU, ending an era of world politics, has forced these trends to expose their real political character – has forced them into the counter-revolutionary pro-imperialist camp.

Uphold the banner of communism!

Capitalism is incapable of solving the vast problems of poverty, inequality and economic underdevelopment confronting the overwhelming majority of humanity. Neo-liberal solutions – privatisation and the free reign of market forces – have already created a catastrophy for the peoples of the third world. They now threaten the same for the working class of the former socialist camp. In the imperialist countries unemployment, poverty and homelessness are growing. The class struggle must therefore continue.

Despite the huge setbacks and demoralisation of recent years communists have a duty to work towards the reconstitution of a genuine non-sectarian communist movement. Such a movement will be internationalist, anti-imperialist and will break with the reactionary traditions of social democracy. The Revolutionary Communist Group calls on all those – organisations and individuals – who have opposed the counter-revolution in the socialist bloc to come together to discuss the formation of a new communist movement in Britain. Such a movement is necessary as part of an international process of studying, learning and acting upon the lessons of the socialist experience since 1917. There can be little justification in the present critical period for socialists of different political trends refusing to unite around a common internationalist, anti-imperialist platform. ∎